THE PROPHETS AND ISRAEL'S CULTURE

THE UNIVERSITY OF CHICAGO PRESS
CHICAGO, ILLINOIS

—

THE BAKER & TAYLOR COMPANY
NEW YORK

THE CAMBRIDGE UNIVERSITY PRESS
LONDON

THE MARUZEN-KABUSHIKI-KAISHA
TOKYO, OSAKA, KYOTO, FUKUOKA, SENDAI

THE COMMERCIAL PRESS, LIMITED
SHANGHAI

THE PROPHETS
AND ISRAEL'S CULTURE

By

WILLIAM CREIGHTON GRAHAM

Professor of Old Testament Language and Literature
The University of Chicago

THE UNIVERSITY OF CHICAGO PRESS
CHICAGO · ILLINOIS

TO MY WIFE

FOREWORD

It is only recently that biblical scholars have become socially minded. For centuries they combined scriptural texts into an oracular theology. A couple of generations ago they began literary criticism, analyzing biblical books, determining the time and place of their composition, their probable authorship, and their editorial combination. In no field has there been more, if indeed, as much minute examination of literature. But literary criticism gave no appreciation of religion as a form of social behavior. It is, of course, true that elaborate studies were made in what was called the historical background of literature and into this background the literature was ingeniously set. The influence of Egypt, Assyria, and Babylon was recognized in the development of religious institutions and gods but, as one who has had some part in this type of literary study, I have to confess that it left me cold. However important the knowledge of the documents and however satisfactory might be the fitting of literature into the history of the Near East, the result was encyclopedic rather than religious. We came to know a deal about Biblical literature and gained a vast amount of information about Hebrew religion, but we did not really get at the Hebrew religion as it was actually practiced by the people themselves. In consequence the critical study of the Bible did not make a contribution to the religious life of today commensurate with the industry of the critics. Its interest was in a literature rather than in people.

In the case of archaeology the results for a time appeared to be much the same. The importance of its early results can hardly be overestimated. They served to check and give bases for literary and historical processes. They did, indeed, give something more. They brought one to the actual life of actual people. But archaeology like criticism is a handmaid rather than a mistress. However much the defender of the Bible has been able to utilize the results of excavations in Biblical lands, too often archaeological interest exhausted itself in the curiosity of visitors to a museum. In archaeology as in the literary criticism the perception of religion as a phase of a total social situation was too often lacking.

But a new epoch in the study of religion is opening. Within the last few years it has passed from literature and archaeological remains to the reconstruction of actual life processes of people who have organized religions. Thus religion is seen to be an aspect of developing culture, the patterns of which it uses in organizing the religious behavior of the masses. As its relation to cultures was genetic, religious development was genetic. Anthropology which for a while seemed to throw the shackles of primitivity over religion now places it as a form of social behavior in its proper perspective. Particularly is this true in the work of my colleagues in the Department of Oriental Languages and Literature in the University of Chicago. With unparalleled opportunity for the discovery of ancient cultures, archaeology and literary criticism to them have for their goal, not the accumulation of relics in a museum or the analysis of documents, but a better knowledge of the origin of civilization and particularly the development of morality and religious behavior. Without the detailed work of the last fifty years in literary criticism and archaeological discovery this reconstruction of the religious experiences of the Hebrew people would have been impossible.

But it is one thing to arrive at a knowledge of the literature and even the practices of a religious group and another to appreciate the reasons for such practices and the motives for emphasis upon the religious teaching which biblical literature preserves. That task calls for genuine historical method and social psychology. The general connection of the Hebrew people with the Semitic stock and of certain elements of the Hebrew religion with rites and institutions of older faiths is no novelty but the struggle of the religious leaders among the Hebrews with their social environment is, thanks to the work of Professor Graham, now taking on new life and meaning. They are seen to be less innovators than transformers of religion. We see their efforts to interpret the dangers and to arouse the ideals of their people as no longer alien to our day. The Biblical literature, especially of the prophets, takes on a dramatic quality which the most meticulous literary study never gave. We see them facing problems which every religious reformer in some shape or other has had to face. The emergence of one social group from the influence of an existing culture, the development of reforms which protect personal values, the emancipation of ideals from inherited religious practices and the control of outworn religious ideas and customs, the struggle to rectify economic conditions rooted in social inheritances, the sublimation of old cultural patterns into motives for the direction of new social situations—these are no strangers to the religious life of today. The backward pull of animalism and of privilege entrenched in social inequality and injustice, the need of a God who is more than a traditional formula, the organization of religion on moral rather than magical bases become in this social appreciation of the Hebrew religion intensely human.

This social phase in biblical study will go far to bridge the chasm which has unfortunately developed between a proper understanding of the Bible and religious education. For intelligent persons, the Bible in ceasing to be oracular too often has become a sort of cross-word puzzle in literary study. From the point of view represented by Professor Graham it becomes an inspiring record of struggles which illustrate the age-long quest for a better life in which our day as well as the past participates.

SHAILER MATHEWS

UNIVERSITY OF CHICAGO

ACKNOWLEDGMENTS

One is naturally inclined to be diffident about making acknowledgments for a publication which has yet to pass the judgment of a learned and critical audience. This is especially the case with a very modest volume, such as the present, which seeks, in brief and non-technical fashion, to place before the thoughtful layman in the field with which it deals an interpretation of the part played by the prophets in the evolution of Israel's culture. The fact that the methodology employed in the underlying studies is, in some respects, a departure from that commonly employed in the past increases one's reticence and compels the explicit absolution, from responsibility for the published results, of all those from whom one has derived direct stimulation.

One who has enjoyed for nearly nine years the inestimable privilege of fellowship with the faculty and student body of the University of Chicago is at a loss to know where to begin in acknowledging the manifold influences which have quickened his mind and helped toward the maturing of his understanding.

Grateful acknowledgments are due to all one's colleagues in the Department of Oriental Languages and Literatures, and more especially to Professor J. H. Breasted, Director of the Oriental Institute, to the late Professors J. M. P. Smith and D. D. Luckenbill, and to Professors M. Sprengling and A. T. Olmstead for whatever is here displayed of ability to see the Hebrews in relation to that larger Near Eastern world in which they were so intimately and fatefully involved.

To Dean Emeritus Shailer Mathews and all his colleagues in the Divinity School, but more especially to Dean S. J. Case, the late Professor G. B. Smith, and Professors A. E. Haydon and C. W. Gilkey, to Dean Gordon J. Laing of the Humanities Division, University of Chicago, and to Professor T. J. Meek, of the University of Toronto, one is indebted for much of whatever soundness of methodology, of viewpoint, and of insight may have found its way into these pages.

Last, but far from least, one acknowledges the contributions of those students and friends, notably Professor H. G. May, of Oberlin Graduate School of Theology, which have been made in the bonds of the fellowship which grows up between those who see a task to be done and strive together to fit themselves for the doing of it. Most of all one hopes that they will not be too much disappointed in the contents of these pages.

To Miss Mary D. Alexander thanks are due for assistance with the preparation of the manuscript for the press and for the reading of the proofs, and to Mr. Louis F. Bernstein for assistance in the making of the Index.

Beyond all these is the contribution acknowledged in the dedication.

WILLIAM CREIGHTON GRAHAM

UNIVERSITY OF CHICAGO
August 25, 1934

TABLE OF CONTENTS

PART I. THE WORLD

PART II. THE PROPHETS

CONCLUSION

BIBLIOGRAPHY

INDEX

PART I
THE WORLD

CHAPTER I

THE WORLD AND ITS WAY

By its very etymology the term "culture" has a religious coloring. A culture is something more than just a way of living. It is a way which is distinguished by attentiveness to the total scene in which life is lived. This quality, which is of the essence of culture, this quality for which the *cultus* properly stands, it is religion's proper function to contribute. Religion, then, is the matrix of culture. Any really non-religious way is a negligent way, just as any really attentive way is to some extent a religious way. And a negligent way of life, a way which develops no inherent significance as a way, does not deserve to be dignified as a culture.

It is well that one should be ready to recognize that the forces which initiate and in the rough determine the pattern of a culture are not, properly speaking, religious forces. Of these forces the physical habitat itself is perhaps the most basic. Certainly this is the case in the earlier stages of human development before man's capacity to cope with his natural environment becomes very considerable. But even in these stages the human factor, the innate and ever increasing human genius for techniques, exercises a most potent influence on culture. The instruments man invents, as he follows the bent of his genius for relating himself successfully to nature, also condition and determine the major features of his life.

When any society has responded to the full to these

conditioning factors, when it has worked out the economic and political aspects of the way of life as nature and human skill seem to dictate, still, until something more than this is done, that culture is but embryonic, has not yet been brought to birth. It is in this bringing of the culture to birth that religion, which is the mother of culture, plays the chief rôle. For it is religion which concerns itself with the integration of the emerging economic and political forces into an order which promises satisfaction. That is always religion's function—to point the way to the highest satisfactions which are attainable in a way of life which promises some measure of stability. Religion does not merely rationalize any newly emerging way of life. It seeks rather to discern what capacities for human happiness and satisfaction are inherent in it. It endeavors to relate such forces to the ongoing human quest for the more abundant and secure life. When, through the offices of religion, that particular way of life has developed a philosophy of life, or in other words has shaped itself into what are, to those who participate in it, meaningful patterns, then the result may be described as a culture.

In illustration of this one might allude to the fact that the way of life, which is at present emerging in every part of the world which has become industrialized through the modern advance in mechanical engineering, has not yet been brought to birth, has not yet fallen into meaningful patterns. The meaning of the machine in terms of human satisfaction is still a subject upon which there is the widest possible divergence of opinion. If one wishes today to savor the meaning of the word "culture" one must visit remoter areas which have not yet been very much affected by the new economic, political, and social forces which the machine age has unleashed. In such all but un-ruffled cultural backwaters one will find folk who live as those who know what they are to do and why they are to do it, folk who are serenely sure that life is meaningful. But once one pushes out again into the main stream of life, where these new forces play upon one, all sense of such serenity is lost as one is tossed about by conflicting desires, antithetical philosophies, and warring ethics. Here there are patterns of a sort dictated by economic, political, and social expediency. But they are not mean-ingful patterns. The way of life for this age has not yet been brought to birth. The modern world awaits a culture worthy of its genius and summons those whose particular responsibility it is to discern the meaning of life for this age to this all important task.

It is precisely because the Hebrew prophets lived and functioned in a period of cultural transition somewhat similar to that which prevails over large areas of the world's surface today that one who recognizes at all the importance of culture, and of the part religion has histori-cally played in the achievement of it, may find it useful to study them. But before this can be done profitably the main outlines of the history of culture in the world in which they lived must be suggested.

Canaan, as the land in which the great prophets were later born and lived was known to the ancients, was but a very tiny part of a larger geographical area which approx-imated in extent what is today included in the term "Near East." Though limited in area, its position was highly central. It lay at the center of the ancient Near East which, in its turn, lay at the center of the land masses of the Eastern Hemisphere, or, as the prehistorians call it, "The Old World."

Even in remote prehistoric time nature had already constituted the Near East a geographical unit. It was comparatively isolated even then by the presence along its northerly and easterly margins of a zone of heavily forested highlands, while to the west the Mediterranean and to the south the Indian Ocean afforded it much protection. Later on this isolation was increased, especially against the south, as climatic change effected the desiccation of large areas of North Africa and of the so-called "Arabian slab."

In such a land, and especially in more remote southerly sections of it, successive types of man could and did enjoy long ages of cultural homogeneity, of freedom to develop their own attack upon the problem of making a living. The sequence and distribution of human types in the Near East in prehistoric ages is not clearly known. There is increasing reason to believe, from the results of prehistoric archaeology, that Neanderthal man once roamed over much of this area, gaining sustenance by the use of the same type of crudely chipped flint weapons and tools as is associated with him in Europe. After him came modern man of several successive types. The most primitive type, the so-called Eurafrican, lived in a manner very similar to his Neanderthal predecessor, hunting and preparing his food with weapons and tools of a paleolithic fashion.

His successor in the region was Mediterranean man about whose original home controversy still rages. He likewise was a hunter, but his genius for working flint was much greater than that of the Eurafrican who was all but exterminated by Mediterranean man's advance. Though the evidence is capable of several interpretations, it appears likely that Mediterranean man entered the Near East from the north and that he ranged over the whole of this salubrious region, north as well as south of the Mediterranean, making his living by hunting, growing more expert in the flaking of flint, until the crudely chipped nodules with which he began were finally superseded by weapons and tools which constitute the finest examples of pressure-flaked flint artifacts yet discovered.

In this stage of his experience Mediterranean man organized his social life on the family-clan-tribal pattern. That system was well suited to the roving life he followed in those grassy forelands. Had conditions remained as they had been when his ancestors left their cruder weapons and tools beside what are now the dry beds of streams which once drained an affluent Sahara and a richly vegetated Arabia, he might have remained in this way of life indefinitely.

The first step away from this hunting culture was possibly stimulated by the increasing aridity and the resultant scarcity of wild game. The answer to that threat was found in the domestication of animals. The hunter became a keeper of herds and flocks and learned to do battle with his neighbors when necessary for the pastures and increasingly rare streams, springs, and wells which kept these life-sustaining beasts alive. In the more barren areas the cultural evolution halted at that point. The way of the nomadic pastoralist settled into a hard-and-fast but, for him, meaningful pattern, which organized social life under a patriarchal tribalism that was capable of yielding certain very definite values through the fellowship which the individual enjoyed with tribal brothers who were visibly as dependent upon him as he was upon them.

Only in the ever dwindling fertile lands that lay along the margins of great rivers which were periodically replenished by the melting of mountain snows, or in lands which enjoyed a dependable rainfall, was this nomadic hunting-pastoral way of life superseded by virtue of human intelligence and inventiveness by another way of life. How early agriculture developed in the Near Eastern world is not known; but it seems likely that it was the congestion of men and domesticated animals in these more fertile areas, as the process of desiccation continued its ruthless progress, which stimulated men to the supplementation of the means of support by the cultivation of trees and plants.

At the dawn of history agriculture is already established in the naturally fertile areas, and its possibilities as a way of life have already seized upon the imagination and stimulated the inventive and organizing genius of man to such an extent that economic and political forces have been released which are on the way to exercising a very profound effect upon social structures and upon human character. For already, in the most dependably fertile of the good lands, the capacity to produce the sustaining goods of life has reached the point where surpluses are possible. The creation of these surpluses has vastly complicated life. Human inventiveness has been called upon to discover ways and means of dealing with them. The invention of pottery helped to solve that problem. The evolution of the walled city, as a safe depositary for such stores, was another answer to it. The growing demand for organizing ability and the increasing call for the manufactured accessories of safety and comfort resulted in more and more complex differentiations of labor. In short, with the discovery of a way of life by which the sustenance of all could be produced by the labor of some, human inventiveness was more and more stimulated to find ways and means of increasing, enriching, and perpetuating the material symbols of a satisfying order of life.

Driven by this passion for insuring materialistic satisfactions into an increasingly complex way of life, and stimulated in the same direction by repeated intrusions of marginal peoples into their affluent lands, the settled and more highly civilized peoples of the Near East began to find it necessary to build up larger and more complex social integrations. The basis of the city state, the monarchy, and the empire, which here in turn succeeded the more primitive tribal patriarchalism, was the emergence of gifted and daring individuals. That, it must be remembered, is something else than a true doctrine of individualism. The social transition which took place here was from one kind of socialism to another, from a socialism based upon intimate personal relationships and visible mutual interdependence to a socialism based upon autocratic authority, on a doctrine, not of the rights and responsibilities of the individual, but of the rights and responsibilities of certain individuals. So far as the individual as such was concerned he was, on the theory that it was for his own good, more suppressed than ever he had been before. The individual had placed himself in the hands of certain individuals who proceeded then to regiment his desires, his ideas, and his conduct for the perpetuation of the prerogatives thus reposed in themselves.

The inevitable result was an age-long struggle for power between great individualists who insisted that most of their contemporaries should remain socialists. That, for example, is the significance of David's clash with Nabal of Carmel.[1] It was a case of the greater individualist crushing the lesser. Down to the appearance of the great Hebrew prophets, the Near Eastern world lived upon the hope of the emergence of the great individual. Nor can it be of small significance that that was an age when economic and political rivalries resulted in more and more constant and sanguine warfare.

It is clear, then, that in a certain sense the Near East is a cultural unit. By that one means that, during the first two stages of cultural evolution, the hunting and animal husbandry stages, there was a common culture all over the area that is so denoted. It is true that in the more arid areas the cultural evolution was halted at this point and remained static. But the higher cultures which emerged in the fertile areas can only be understood if one remembers that the agricultural peoples came originally from the same cultural situation as that in which the nomadic peoples remained. Later, when these nomadic peoples intrude into the higher cultures of the settled lands, they find many points of affinity between the philosophy of their own culture and that into which they intrude.

[1] I Sam. 25:1–43.

These facilitate their accommodation to the new pattern of life, while the contrasts, which are at the same time encountered, work simultaneously against complete conformity. The conflicts thus set up within the spirits of the intruders result in cultural struggle through which they and their descendants made their great contribution to the civilization of the settled lands.

Since religion is the mother of culture it is not at all surprising to find that the Near East is also a religious unit. Each stage of the cultural evolution was accompanied by a corresponding evolution of religion. As in the case of culture, so also in the case of religion, the early stages of the evolution were, in their main features, the same all over the area, and each successive stage carried over survivals from the preceding one.

Again, as in the case of culture, this evolution of religion was halted in the barren lands where religion remained relatively static for long centuries. Only in the fertile areas were new elements more rapidly and lavishly added to surviving features of outmoded religious patterns, so that here the normal trend of religion, like the trend of life itself, was toward complexity.

One is not to conclude from this that the forces of religion were simply lagging behind and conforming to the dictates of economic and political forces. One must see this religious process as an essentially sincere attempt to interpret life as it was, and as a sincere effort to make the most of it. Yet all the way through this general Near Eastern religious evolution there can be traced the same fundamental philosophy of life, the same all but universally accepted judgments of life's values, the same con-

ception of the nature of the world, and the same attitude
to institutions. It was on this general background that
there finally appeared, faintly at first, but with growing
clarity, the tracings of a different religious pattern, the
dawning of a different philosophy of life. One must first
turn, however, to consideration of the general religious
evolution before one is in a position to understand that
particular deviation from it for which Israel's prophets
are so largely responsible.

One returns then to the time when the primitive ancestors of the basic stock of most of the later peoples of
the Near East were ranging that great area, gaining their
sustenance chiefly from its wild life. The outstanding
condition of life in the hunting stage is man's absolute dependence on nature. He thinks of it as a "vast immensity
wherein resides a vague and veiled power" which is of
quite another category than himself. This diffused superforce lies behind all visible forms, and the beasts on whom
man must live are closer to it than he is. They are Nature's "first-born children." And man, in order to be able
to live, must curry the favor of this superforce. He de-
vises ceremonies to cajole it and to placate the beasts
which he must kill. The art of certain paleolithic caves
consists of representations of animals. These caves were
shrines wherein these rites were performed.

This primitive idea of an impersonal superforce which
man may use through secret techniques in the pursuit of
his own desires is the root of magic and taboo. It lies also
at the root of totemism, which is thought by many au-
thorities to develop from the individual's worship of his
animal guardian spirit, the identity of which was usually

revealed to him in a trance superinduced by vigil and fasting. Survivals of this animal worship stage may be noted in the ancient literatures of all the peoples of this region including the Hebrews. But this heritage from the hunting stage of cultural evolution is most prominent in the religion of Egypt.

The idea of animal guardian spirits opened the way for an animistic view of nature. In this stage men come to regard every manifestation of nature as the work of a spirit. Trees, streams, springs, stones, rocks, and mountains are inhabited each by a particular spirit. From animism to polytheism is but a step reflecting man's growing appreciation of personality. The spirit or demon has no individuality but the gods and goddesses have. Each of them has special attributes and functions in the economy of nature. They are anthropomorphically conceived, and are named. But no one of them is ever conceived to be cosmic in the true sense. The primitive gods are adjuncts to man's life. They are not moral beings. They have no purposes, have only limited intelligence, and are highly capricious.

That all reflects primitive man's experience with his world. It was a capricious place at best. The goddess of the soil might bless his sowing, or the god of the shepherd enlarge the flock, only to have the god of the storm or drought destroy it all. Through all this long development the idea of the remote impersonal superforce of another category persisted. Behind all the gods, however conceived, there was still the ultimate power which man, if he had the secret, could use to bend the gods to his will. The gods were potential helpers, and more and more as man perfected his adjustment to nature, he believed in his power to influence the gods.

As long as the world was the scene of the operations of so many deities it was hard to work out a system of life. Perhaps one should put it the other way around and say that until a system of life was worked out, this confusing polydemonistic or polytheistic world-view was bound to obtain. Agriculture opened the way toward a simpler and more orderly world-view.

The emergence of this mode of life meant some great changes in human thinking and conduct. The attitude to Nature changed as man saw in himself a factor which exercised some control over her economy. Woman, who probably was the discoverer and early developer of this way of making a living, came to have a much more important place in the social scheme. As men ceased to rove and settle down she became the stable, productive element. In some such way as this men came to see the earth as a female principle, the Mother of life.

In the primitive agricultural communities society was organized around a cult in which the chief divinities were the Earth Mother and her Son-Consort who personified the vegetative life which springs from her. In these communities the ruling power was exercised not by the chief, but by the priest, who knew the magic by which the annual cycle of life was maintained. This was a simple peasant religion of productivity, and, though there were other gods who exercised other functions, this fertility triad held the larger place in the thought and affections of the people.

When the Hebrews entered Canaan the society of that

land was organized around a more elaborate and complex version of that primitive peasant cult. The increased production of wealth had made possible the emergence of the city state. The chief had become a king and by supplanting the priest had come to be the chief religious personage, being regarded as an incarnation of the Earth Mother's Son-Consort. Growing concern with the seasonal cycle and the relation of the earth to the heavenly bodies had brought about the addition of solar, lunar, and astral features to the cultus, although with most men the earth gods still commanded the greatest interest.

This pattern was accepted all over the agricultural world, from the Tigris-Euphrates Valley, where the Sumerians, Akkadians, and their successors had long since worked out their own version of it, through Assyria, where at the lowest level of the site of ancient Assur the excavators found a temple to Mother Earth, on into Asia Minor, where this peasant religion is found in its simplest and most unchanged form down to the Christian era. Turning south down through North Syria the same cult appears. From Ras Shamra within the last few years have come the texts of myths and rituals which show that between 1300 and 1800 B.C. this was the religious pattern of the Phoenician region. If, for the moment, one skips Canaan and passes over to Egypt one finds it very prominent there in the Osiris-Isis-Horus cult. Even if there were no evidence on this point in the Old Testament itself, the conclusion is unavoidable that Canaan could not have escaped the influence of this pattern of culture. It has, of course, long been known that the Baalism which so exercised the prophets was of the same type. What has not been sufficiently appreciated is that it, and not the religion of the prophets, shaped the prevailing pattern of culture in Canaan for centuries after the Hebrew entry.

It is exceedingly important to remember that these ancient Near Eastern folk, from long habit, expressed their philosophy of life through the medium of the myths and rituals which arose within the cultus of the dominant religion. The folk tale, which often borrowed motifs from the current mythology, was another vehicle.

By the time the Hebrews entered Canaan, as the Ras Shamra finds make abundantly clear, the peoples who lived along the Syro-Palestinian seaboard were already in the enjoyment of a fairly complex body of mythology and quite elaborate cultus rituals based upon the mythology. But though the mythology was by now fairly complex the central myth, which formed a nexus to which other myths were ancillary, was in that part of the world where masses and classes alike were still visibly dependent for sustenance upon the fertility of flock, herd, orchard, and field, the ancient myth of the Earth Mother and her Son-Consort.

The great religious moments of these people were those feasts which marked the major phases of the seasonal cycle. The ceremonies conducted on these great festal occasions were dramatizations of the cult myth which detailed the life-story of the consort of Mother Earth. The myth naturally varies in different localities, but the principal motifs are the same through most variations. These are: the death of the god, symbolizing autumn; his descent to the nether world, symbolizing winter; the descent of the goddess in search of her consort, her struggle with the forces which imprison him, his final return with her to earth and the marriage of the divine pair, symbolizing spring and the fruits of summer.

Aside from these great occasions, the operations of daily life were governed by the same cycle of ideas. When the peasant worked his ground or pruned his vines there were rituals fitting to the occasion. The Hebrew verb "to prune" means also "to chant." A lot of the cult words of the Hebrews came over from this older culture. With the words they took over the system itself and the whole form of literary expression is influenced by the symbols of the cult. When the prophets long afterward come to criticize the system they can only make themselves intelligible by employing these same symbols.

As one looks back over the almost constant economic and political pressures to which Canaan was subjected, one is not surprised to find that its religion was one which focused men's desires on the production and accumulation of material wealth. Almost constantly under the thumb of imperial masters, it was inevitable that its people should seek some measure of security through the creation of a surplus. It was easy to confuse the means with the end and to make productivity an end in itself.

It is true that they set a high value on affection in personal relationships. But love, as they knew it and pursued it, was almost wholly a physical satisfaction, a craving for creature comfort which had to be gratified just as hunger and thirst, and which was itself motivated by the urge to reproduce.

Because, in this society, human desire was held by the system at the physical level it became easily prey to those, within and without, who knew how to exploit the physical appetites.

The idea of reality in this system matched up with the range of values. By emphasizing material values men came to see the world as nothing more than the scene of a struggle for physical existence. Though they believed in gods their world-view was materialistic. Their gods were aspects of nature mythicized, and were never conceived as truly cosmic beings. Though they did not realize the implications of their own attitudes to the gods, the ultimate power did not reside in deities who were themselves subject to human control. Implicit in this world-view was the idea that there was no mind or purpose in the world higher than that which was manifest in man himself. The superforce was impersonal, non-intelligent, non-purposive. It could be used but there could be no other relationship with it.

This early Canaanite knew little about his world and still less about himself. Of himself he knew little except the physical appetites which clamored for satisfaction. Of his latent mental powers, of his unsuspected capacity for aspiration toward fuller satisfactions, he knew little. He had not yet awakened to the glory of his selfhood, and could not become conscious of the implications such an awakening would suggest concerning the real nature of his world.

He was at school beginning to learn about his world by a painful process of trial and error. He had progressed to the extent of realizing that there was a cycle of order of some sort in nature. True, it was not a very dependable order; but he was learning, in spite of his conceit of coercion, to co-operate with it. The lesson to which he had set himself man has not yet learned. The conceit of control and coercion of nature still moves him. Most of the ills to which he is prey spring from a perverse endeavor to coerce forces with which he should be striving rather to co-operate.

That brings one naturally to an evaluation of the religious technique which most people followed. This matched up with the range of values and the world-view. Since men desired material satisfactions in a world which might not be depended upon, but was subject to coercion, the way to live was to accept the authority of those who possessed the secret of coercion.

That was a comfortable way to live because one did not have to think for one's self. One accepted a system and conformed to it. So long as life ran smoothly enough that was very well. But manners and customs became deeply fixed by habit. Institutions tended to adhere rigidly to the accepted mold. Life became static, the swiftly passing years a series of similar cycles. Aspiration and divine discontent were stifled.

In such a system the development of personality was retarded. A man must desire, think, and act as his fathers had before him. His institutions were of more importance than he. The sacrosanctity of his institutions conspired to frustrate his pursuit of reality and to confine his desires to physical levels.

Such, then, was the culture which had dominated Canaan from time immemorial, and which still dominated masses and classes alike when the great prophets of Israel appeared upon the scene. In a world devoted to production they rose to speak of distribution. Into a world committed by habit to a way which carried hoary and venerable religious sanctions, but which was patently inadequate, they came to stimulate men to seek for higher satisfactions under some more perfect order.

CHAPTER II

ISRAEL IN THE WAY OF THE WORLD

It is surely a fact of no little significance that the more adept men become at making a living the more difficult it is to live. Each generation must, so it seems, face the perennial paradox that the more man gains control over his natural environment the harder it is for him to order his relationships with his fellows. It was this paradox, manifestly symptomatic of some deep-seated maladjustment in humanity's life, which engaged the attention of Israel's prophets. As religious men, by habitude attentive to the whole of which they formed a seemingly insignificant part, they felt an irresistible compulsion to deal with this strange flaw in the cosmos.

Their concern with the problem was intensified by the fact that they were members of a social group which, as a result of its failure to find an adequate solution for it, almost constantly faced the final loss of its significance as a group. That impressed upon them deeply that the solution was not to be arrived at by a process of mere adjustment of part to part. Israel had tried that path. It had walked in the world's way with no other result than to find itself in the way of the world and, therefore, about to be eliminated, to become the helpless victim of an economic and political determinism against which there seemed, on the surface of things, to be no appeal.

It should, then, help one to understand why the prophets were driven to plunge deep beneath the surface to find some solution for the problem which faced Israel in their times, if one could, through a historical survey of the movement of economic and political forces in the Near Eastern world, be enabled to enter into their experience of the pressures and tensions amid which they lived. For while the prophets themselves could not have described the origin and nature of these pressures and tensions as may be done today by one who interests himself in Near Eastern history, one must not overlook the part that the experience of the race plays in shaping the psychology of the individual. Whether they knew history or not, they felt it.

It has already been suggested that Nature, in setting the Near Eastern stage, had determined that this area should for long be a world unto itself. Through its relative isolation from the rest of the "Old World," and through its centrality therein, it became the scene of the rise of a higher culture and the focus into which hinterland peoples naturally moved. Oriented on the salubrious Mediterranean, its westward connections were bound to become more important than its eastward contacts.

The determining influence of this Mediterranean orientation on Near Eastern life was intensified by the fact that Nature had decreed that within this world, in extreme opposite corners of it, there should be two distinct poles of power. Along its hilly northern and eastern margins she had flung a broad fertile valley, which was cut in a great figure 8 by the Tigris and Euphrates rivers, themselves a gift from the northern hills to the plain. As if determined to give warning to the encroaching Sahara, on the far southwest, she cast across its eastern reaches the blue ribbon of the Nile, linking it with far-distant equatorial lakes and the turbulent, silt-bearing torrents of Abyssinian hills. These two valleys thus became the only areas within the Near East which were endowed by Nature with the capacity for supporting dense populations in a settled existence. The great concentrations of human beings and of material wealth were bound to be there. They were the poles of power and, once connected, currents of political and economic influence would inevitably pass and repass between them.

The land of Canaan lay directly on the line of tension between these poles of power. It was at the very center of the larger area which was, in its turn, the nexus of the land masses of the "Old World." Not only so, but it constituted a narrow strip of fertile and semi-fertile land which was open, on the one side, to the Arabian Desert and, on the other side, to the great sea. Not far to the north of it loomed, moreover, the great highland barrier of the Taurus. It was from and through these places that there periodically came intrusions into the settled lands which again and again affected the course of history. Canaan, therefore, lay not merely on the path where great indigenous political groups moving in opposite directions clashed, but it also lay in that part of the settled lands which was most open to access by intruders from more backward regions. It was destined, then, to be a focal point of social stress of every kind. A summarization of the political and economic history of the world to which it was so intimately related may throw this statement into sharper relief.

Looked at in the large the political and economic history of man in the ancient Near East may be briefly characterized as consisting of two periods of imperialism separated by an interlude of self-determination.

As the historical age dawns the Near Eastern world is still very far from having achieved anything like an empire. Not only is it yet relatively isolated from the rest of the world but its various parts are comparatively isolated from each other. Communication is local and indirect. The centers of power in the two great valleys touch each other only through lesser intermediaries. They are each of them very much occupied with internal affairs. They are only just out of the small city-state stage of political evolution and newly arrived in the monarchical stage. Both valleys are divided north against south. The achievement of anything approaching internal unity has yet to be accomplished. The Near Eastern world seems still to lack some stimulus that will make it conscious of itself as a whole.

The stimulus which will finally have this effect ultimately comes, not from within, but from without. Aryan tribesmen from the far north penetrate the highland barrier late in the third millennium B.C., and, aided by certain technological advantages, become dominant in a fusion with the indigenous Armenoid highlanders and with Semitic man. By the eighteenth century B.C. North Syria is under the control of this fusion. Another hundred years sees it in control of the eastern littoral of the Mediterranean and beginning to send immigrants into Egypt. Early in the seventeenth century it conquers Egypt, which it holds subject for approximately a century.

This intrusion ultimately had a tremendous effect on

Near Eastern political and economic life. As a result of it Egyptian imperialism came to birth. The Egyptians under Ahmose I ejected the intruders from Egypt in the first half of the sixteenth century. By the time they had regained control of their own valley they had begun to learn that the good old days of comparative isolation were over. For these enemies, "these Asiatics" as the records call them, merely fell back on Canaan. There could be no security for Egypt as long as an enemy powerful enough to invade her held the lands along the eastern Mediterranean coast. Motivated by a passion for security, Egyptian imperialism begins with an effort to control that coast.

The imperialistic attitude of Egypt toward Asia lasted with varying fortunes from the middle of the sixteenth into the first quarter of the thirteenth century. As imperialism frequently does, it began very auspiciously because the ultimate cost of the adventure was not appreciated. The very physical features of the terrain Egypt had conquered made the control of it a most difficult task. The price of maintaining political stability along the eastern littoral of the Mediterranean was out of all proportion to the cost. The situation was aggravated, too, by the threat to the sovereignty of other nations which was inherent in Egyptian imperialism. When the Pharaoh's columns reached North Syria they were at the foothills of the Taurus, on the one side, and at the head of the Tigris-Euphrates Valley, on the other. The Hittites of Asia Minor saw and accepted this challenge. Babylonia and Assyria watched the west with wary eye and pondered on ways and means to halt its aggressions. The Hittites were especially active and successful at first in disputing Egyptian authority. Their stubborn resistance made the imperialistic venture cost too much.

With the turn of the fourteenth century there is a significant change in Egyptian foreign policy. Diplomacy and subsidy supplant the sword. The first half of the century finds exhausted Egypt unable to cope effectively with any of the greater northern powers, and equally unable to control its own vassal states. It was probably during this period of decline, in what is frequently referred to as "the Amarna age," that the earliest of those settlers, who afterward become known as the Hebrews, entered Canaan.

About the middle of the fourteenth century, with the accession of the nineteenth dynasty, there is a revival of the imperialistic spirit in Egypt and the old struggle with the Hittites is renewed. But the final result of this flare-up is a stalemate which passes, in 1272 B.C., by solemn treaty, into an alliance for offense and defense between these hereditary enemies. This Hittite-Egyptian alliance is most significant. It is called into being by the rapid development between 1350 B.C. and 1272 B.C. of Assyrian power. Imperial expansion by the Egyptians has had the inevitable effect of evoking another imperial structure to check its power. The Egyptian-Hittite alliance, as a deliberate measure to establish a balance of power, is a confession of the strength of the rising Assyrian empire. But that alliance is even more significant as marking the time when a completely self-conscious Near Eastern world comes into existence. Contact between the opposing poles of power is now directly established, though still under control. The two great powers at the opposite extremities are fully aware of each other, and are measuring each other with an eye to conflict under the stimulus of their respective economic necessities.

How long this balance of power might have been able to maintain the equilibrium between these great political forces it is difficult to say. As so often happens in such cases the whole structure falls to pieces about the end of the thirteenth century through the intrusion into the situation of a completely new factor. This is caused by another successful irruption of northern man from beyond the great highland barrier. It begins as a gradual and more or less peaceful penetration. Its success is due in part to certain technological superiorities, particularly the possession of the secrets of producing iron, and of the fabrication of armor. About 1200 B.C. these new men of the north completely destroy the Hittite power and all but succeed in conquering Egypt. The Western alignment of powers, which had held the balance of power from 1272 to 1200 B.C., is completely broken. The reverberations of this disturbance have an almost equally disastrous effect on the Eastern powers. Assyrian imperialism is effectively checked from 1200 B.C. to 900 B.C. Not till then can Assyria again give really effective consideration to the West.

For these three centuries, then, from 1200–900 B.C. there exists, relatively speaking, an interlude of imperial quiescence. The two great valleys are very much preoccupied with their own concerns. The peoples of all the intermediate territory are thus, to all intents and purposes, left to determine their destiny among and for themselves. The Nordic newcomers are as yet unfitted to assume the full burden of government. They are no more than a loosely organized tribal conglomeracy, unable to unify themselves, much less the people of the lands they overrun. They break up and settle wherever necessity dictates as, for example, the Philistine group subsides on the southern end of the eastern Mediterranean coast. The peoples of Syria and Canaan now have to adjust themselves to these newcomers without recourse to the controlling interest of any great world-power. There has been a short circuit on the line between the Near East's two great poles of power, its two great valleys, and in that in-between region power has to set up new poles for itself.

The Nordic newcomers have a great advantage. Local groups, like the Hebrew clansmen, are at a loss in dealing with them because of their superiority in the crafts. It is a time of severe testing for these older stocks. They must of themselves and for themselves find a way of withstanding the invader or become slaves. The issue is long in doubt and in most instances the turn it takes depends largely on individuals. Among the Hebrews a series of great individuals, Samuel, Saul, David, Jonathan, and Joab rise to lead their people through a stage of social transition from the city state to the genuine monarchy into relative freedom and independence.

It is easy to see the importance of this transition to the Hebrews though its bearing on the life of the modern West is not so obvious. Yet it is true that the Old Testament literature is in large part the record of Israel's experience with the monarchy. The monarchy was accepted as the political instrument most useful for mitigating and controlling the social pressures of that age. The Old Testament records tell much of that phase of Israel's experimentation in search of the good life. That record itself is one which has, through its place in the cultural heritage, influenced the civilization of the West. Of the life behind that record the latter has been in some sense the heir, through the mediation of both Christianity and Judaism. Whatever Western culture may have derived in these ways from that older culture it owes, in a sense, to those northern peoples who came into the Near East about 1200 B.C., broke up the old imperialism, and so opened the way for the Hebrew experiment with the monarchy.

By 900 B.C. the interlude of political self-determination is definitely at an end. This comes about through a change in the general Near Eastern situation which might be described as a revival of imperialism. Though still conscious of the importance of Syria-Palestine to its safety, Egypt's imperial days are now really over. By the age of the Twentieth Dynasty Egypt had passed into priestly control and only occasionally thereafter does it find any forceful leadership. From that time on its political methods are increasingly compounded of intrigue and machination.

From 900 B.C. to the battle of Issus in 333 B.C. the Tigris-Euphrates Valley furnishes, in a series of three great imperial structures, the Assyrian empire down to 612, the Babylonian empire 612–539, and the Persian empire, 539–333, the dominant power in the Near Eastern world. The first two of these are Semitic empires. But with the third, the Persian, domination passes to the

Aryan peoples and remains with them through the Greek and Roman empires till after the rise of Christianity.

All of the three great eastern empires, Assyria, Babylonia, and Persia, endeavor to project themselves into the West. This is inevitable because the Near East is oriented westward. In the West the great prize of imperial ambition is the wealthy valley of the Nile. As long as the seat of imperial power lay in the East, Egypt made use in turn of all the Western peoples including the Hebrews, Syrians, Phoenicians, and Greeks to ward off the Eastern threat. The great Western powers of later times, the Greeks and Romans, are stimulated to rise by these aggressions of the Eastern empire into their sphere of influence, until later on the West comes back into the East to bring about an even more complex and bewildering agglomeration of races and cultures than ever before.

In all this interplay of social stresses and tensions one can catch glimpses of a design which is suggested in the physical conformation of this Near Eastern world. For through the whole vast and variegated area winds a verdurous strip which symbolizes a more abundant life to which every soul on its stoniest hillside or its most arid and sandy waste is entitled. The design contemplates the integration and enrichment of the threads of human life which shuttle ceaselessly back and forth across this corrugated warp of precipitous mountain and verdant valley, of rich plain and desert steppe, of roaring wady and placid, broad-bosomed river. This world must be socially integrated. It must achieve that measure of political and economic unity which its physical conformation demands of it. There will be no stability here until it is in some way unified. And the only way known to those who guide its destinies is the way of economic and political coercion. Here is an attempt at integration based almost entirely on a materialistic philosophy of life, on the assumption that might arises only from the things men produce, never from the personal capacities which enable them to produce them. Control the product, so the doctrine runs, and you may coerce the producer. It is a doctrine which would be true if man were not man, if there were not innate in him needs and capacities which outleap the physical paraphernalia with which he surrounds himself.

In view of this general picture two particular facts become significant. One is that the supreme manifestation of the phenomenon we know as prophecy begins to emerge when this economic and political rivalry is nearing a high peak of intensity. The other is that it takes its rise, not within the society of the great rival powers, but within the society of two small buffer states which lie on the path of these rival powers. In other words it appears within a society where these very pressures create severe internal tensions resulting in glaring social maladjustments.

The nature of these tensions may be rapidly suggested. First of all one may mention the rise of political partisanship from rival ideas of political policy. The Hebrew kingdoms are not united by external pressure, but, on the contrary, political factionalism, with the attendant disposition to intrigue and duplicity, grows apace, a circumstance which bespeaks some deep-seated, moral disintegration.

Again, social contrasts become appalling, as a productive, hard-working peasantry is called upon to support not only a local ruling caste whose standards of living are set by those of their own overlords, but to yield up also its meed of wealth to the insatiable maw of the same overlords. The peasantry of Israel sinks into peonage, while those who rule them are willing to pay even that price for their own very relative economic and political security.

But perhaps the crowning touch in this sordid story, the thing that rouses the ire of the prophets more than anything else, is the fact that the accepted religious leadership, the priests and prophets of the dominant cultus, not only refuse to see what is going on, but acquiesce in it and even profit by it. They lend themselves, in other words, to an exploitive attitude, to an attitude which is a denial of human worth, to an attitude which thrusts the race as a whole back to the brink of bestiality. This callous indifference to humankind, this willingness to profit by its degeneracy, this spiritual meanness of the custodians of culture—this is the "last, unkindest cut of all" which the prophetic soul cannot bear.

Under the stresses and tensions which have just been suggested, Israel's alternatives are limited in number and dilemmic in nature. The economic advantage of the Hebrew people lies with Egypt and their political advantage, for long centuries, with the great empires of the Tigris-Euphrates Valley. Here is a dilemma which can be attacked, to the mind of the practical man of affairs, in one of two ways. The Hebrew kingdoms can co-operate with confederacies of neighboring states which enjoyed the moral support of Egypt, and very little more, against the great Eastern power. This course, especially after the middle of the ninth century, invariably leads to political disaster. Or they can, if they are so minded, place themselves under the "protection" of the great Eastern power and assist in driving Egypt out of Asia. This course invariably leads to economic disaster both because it entails heavy tribute, and because when the roads of Palestine are no longer open to Egyptian traffic that land is left on an economic backwater. The Hebrew leaders vacillate constantly between these two policies. But no matter which one they follow, the result is always the same, economic and political decline. No path to significance lies open to them either through politics or economics. The Hebrew nations, as nations, will ultimately be "broken and snared and taken," as Isaiah puts it.

There is only one path to significance and that is the one the prophets point out—the path which lies through cultural distinctiveness. Only if these people can somehow develop an inherently significant way of life, if they can build up some unique range of desires, some unusual philosophy, some distinctive ethic, in short some philosophy of life the sharing of which will make them brothers, any time, anywhere, under all circumstances, can Israel hope to escape oblivion, to remain an entity, to project itself down the corridors of time as a significant factor in the great human adventure. One does not say that the prophets realized this need and consciously did what they did in order to meet it. One only says that the need was inherent in their situation, that there was no road open to significance save the cultural road.

CHAPTER III

THE PROPHETS AND THE WORLD'S WAY

That any individual, whether he realizes it or not, begins his life under a heavy indebtedness to the culture of which his birth makes him heir is self-evident. The prophets of Israel are no exception to this rule. As one reads them one finds them more or less in revolt against the whole culture pattern of their day and place and, in particular, decidedly critical of the operating cultus of their times. One has constantly to remember that they are not entirely reliable witnesses concerning the values which inhered in the system against which they protested. No one who is plunged by the social pressures of his time into protest and conflict with the dominant pattern ever is entirely reliable.

Within the prevailing system, inadequate though it had become in the declining years of the Hebrew kingdoms, there were certain values which helped to make the prophets what they became. One may pause a moment now to suggest some of these, so that in the end it may become clear that it cannot be claimed that the prophets alone created the distinctive religion-culture out of which both Christianity and Judaism later took their rise. Their contribution lay, in other words, in the influence they exerted upon the accepted way of life and particularly upon the cultus, not in any rival system which they set up within their society.

Perhaps one of the weightiest items of the prophetic in-

debtedness to Israel's culture lies in the fact that their
outlook on life was the religious outlook. They were born
into a world which had already learned the rudiments of
the lesson that the part must relate itself to the whole,
that the negligent life is never an adequate life. They
were born with an interest in God, that is to say, with a
natural tendency to concern themselves with some constructive synthesis of life. That made the capacity for
analysis which they later developed under social pressure
doubly valuable. It enabled them to be critical without
becoming iconoclastic, to be realistic without becoming
cynical, to see life as it was without losing the conviction
that it could be what it ought to be. To the circumstance
that they were born into a religion-culture, no matter how
inadequate—how shot through with superstition and ignorance—that religion-culture was, one must credit the
fact that the prophetic way is a way of faith, a way which
rejects despair, which resists all suggestion that the social
process as a whole can be futile, that man cannot relate
himself successfully to the whole of which he is a part.

Another point upon which the prophets stood under ob-
ligation to the culture pattern against which they reacted
was the peculiarly pungent manner in which they expressed their reaction. Their speech is replete with allusions to the generally accepted pattern of conduct, and
more especially to the myths and rituals and folk tales in
which the popular philosophy expressed itself. To the use
of these symbols, which were current in all circles of their
society, they brought ideas and moods which were in contrast to the ideas and moods commonly conveyed by
them. As one studies these allusions the prophets become

vibrantly alive, men who not only think but feel, men who, because they are trying to deal with souls, can in the same breath resort to argument, to irony, to compassion, to indignation, and to wistful hope. So their language is unique, stimulating, colorful, dynamic, because of the unwonted use they make of the symbols that are current in contemporary speech. No one can adequately appreciate either their thought or the manner of its expression unless he approaches them, not through the religion-culture which long afterward grew in part from their work, but through the religion-culture against which they were in revolt.

In illustration of the pungency which the prophetic language derives through this wealth of allusion to the dominant culture pattern one may recall the famous pun of Isaiah in his Song of the Vineyard (5:7):

way⁵qaw mišpåṭ wᵉhinēh mispåḥ liṣᵉ dåqåh wᵉhinēh ṣᵉ⁵åqåh.

On the surface the striking thing here is the word play. But the pungency of the pun depends even more on the juxtaposition of incongruities, which are denoted by almost identical words. The English translations in no case bring out the allusion which the pun contains to the rites of the accepted cultus. They give the words a social coloring only. The King James translates:

> And he looked for judgment, but behold oppression
> For righteousness, but behold a cry.

Gordon, in the American Translation, comes a little closer to the text, but still sees only an allusion to what one might call a secular situation:

> He looked for justice, but lo! bloodshed,
> For righteousness, but lo! a cry.

Moffat strains to express something of the incongruity and the word play:

> He looked for justice—and lo bloodshed!
> For right—and lo shrieks from the wronged!

But he too sees no cultic allusion in the words.

But that there is an allusion to the sympathetic magic of the cult rites is rendered likely from the preceding context and from the etymology and usage of the words *mispåḥ* and *ṣᵉ⁽åqåh*. A recently discovered text of a Phoenician ritual makes it certain that Isaiah's Vineyard Song is full of allusion to the magical rite of the preparation of the god's vineyard. The word *mispåḥ* comes from a root which means "to pour out." The allusion in it is either to the shedding of sacrificial blood, or to the pouring out of an oblation, or possibly even to sex magic. The word *sᵉ⁽åqåh* in many contexts means, not a cry of actual pain, but a ritualistic cry used in bewailing the dead consort of Mother Earth. The prophet's meaning and something of his word play may be savored if one renders:

> And he looked for magnanimity and, behold—Magic!
> For righteousness, and behold—Ritual!

The religious rites of the dominant cultus are not related to reality. They have no bearing upon the social tension which stimulates Isaiah's criticism.

Or to take another example from the words of a less known and much less understood prophet, Zephaniah. Like Amos he attacks the popular conceit of the "Day of the Lord," a feature of the dominant religion which saw in the return of the spring, with its long hours of daylight, a symbol of the divine will to save Israel. The great spring festival of the rising of the god was the day of light, of health, of happiness, of victory, of prosperity. Zephaniah is driven by the hopelessness of the international situation to see in "the Day of the Lord" no hope but the grim certainty that Yahweh will manifest himself in such a way as to cut the foundations from under the whole order which bases its life on economic power and finds its satisfactions in political rivalry and cruelty. He predicts the downfall of all these heathen nations including Judah, which he finds no better than its neighbors.

In 2:11 there are certain words of the prophet which are translated thus in the King James:

> The Lord will be terrible unto them for he will famish all
> the gods of the earth; and men shall worship him every
> one from his place, even all the isles of the heathen.

Moffat regards the verse as an interpolation, transposes it to follow verse 15, and translates it thus:

> Grimly will the Eternal assail them all;
> For he disables all gods of the earth,
> Till every pagan shore does homage to himself.

Smith, in the American Translation, is much more faithful to the text:

> The Lord will be terrible against them

that is, against these pagan nations, including Judah itself,

> For he will famish all the gods of the earth
> So that there shall bow down to him each from its place
> All the shores of the nations.

In this passage there are expressions which sound strange in modern ears, such as "the famishing of the gods of the earth" and "the bowing down of shores." But when one approaches this verse through a study of the cultus and of its relation to the political order these difficulties vanish. In the recently discovered Ras Shamra texts the fertility god, Alein Baal, who is thought of as controlling life, is described as the one who "makes fat gods and men." In all those kingdoms of the agricultural world the king was regarded as in some sense the incarnation of this god. Kings, if not thought of as actually divine in Zephaniah's time, still claimed divine right. They were the earthly representatives of the god of sustenance and life. Zephaniah is alluding here to these features of the culture pattern and predicting that Yahweh, who to him is the supreme arbiter of destiny, will make lean these "gods" who profess to be able to make their people fat. He is expressing a hope that some catastrophe of cosmic origin may sweep away the economic foundations upon which this cruel and violent political order rests. The verse might be translated thus:

> Terrible will Yahweh be against them!
> For he will make lean all the earth gods.
> O may they bow down to him, each man from his sanctuary,
> All the pagan lusters!

Such are Zephaniah's sentiments toward the divine kings of the nations who in the rituals of the sanctuaries of the time enacted the rôle of the dying and rising god of material productivity.

The attitude of Zephaniah toward the political aspects of the commonly accepted type of cultus is very significant. All the great pre-exilic prophets are characterized by the same refusal to admit the pretensions of kings to divine right. All of them reflect a sense of disillusionment about the type of monarchy which prevailed in their world. It is clear that the generally accepted culture pattern is inadequate to meet either the political or the economic pressures of the time. The world to which the prophets came stood badly in need of a "New Deal."

PART II
THE PROPHETS

CHAPTER IV

THE HEART OF THE PROPHETIC
PHILOSOPHY OF LIFE

At the heart of the prophetic philosophy of life lies a distinctive view of the world. It is easy for one to overlook the contribution of the prophets to the history of human thought. They antedated the formal science of thought. They had no equipment of recognized principles of logic. They spent no consideration on the processes of thought. Whoever understands thinking to be the same as formal ratiocination, whoever is so subservient to the conventions of the formal sciences as to consider that thought is something apart from emotion and will may easily miss almost completely the significance of the intellectual aspects of the ministry of Israel's prophets.

Two circumstances which have attended religious life in recent years have perhaps contributed to the failure to appreciate the prophetic contribution to philosophy. One is the emphasis upon the social gospel which fostered a disposition to consider the prophets almost entirely in relation to the social maladjustments which stimulated their reaction to life. The other is the emphasis on evolution which led to an interest in the growth of the idea of God and resulted in spreading the cynicism that man makes God in his own image. In preoccupation with relating God concepts to an evolutionary social process, interpreters of the prophets are prone to fail to stress the point that the significance of the concept does not arise from the circumstances which stimulate it but from the personality which experiences them and passes judgment on their meaning through his idea of God. Two persons sustain experience of approximately similar circumstances and come out of it with different conceptions of God, that is to say, with different interpretations of the real nature of the totality of things. So the great anonymous prophet of the Babylonian exile addresses his exiled fellow-countrymen thus:

> Why should you say, O Jacob,
> And speak, O Israel:
> "My way is hidden from the Lord
> And my rights are passed over by my God?"
> Have you not known? have you not heard?
> The Lord is a God everlasting,
> The Creator of the ends of the earth.
> He does not faint, nor grow weary;
> His insight is unfathomable.
> He gives power to the fainting,
> And to him that has no might he increases strength.[1]

Here are two widely different reactions to an identical set of circumstances expressed in sharply contrasted ideas of God. Does that mean that man makes God in his own image? Such a judgment is an entirely superficial view of the matter. Here are expressed, not two momentary and entirely contemporary reactions to stimuli, but two views of the nature of the world, two fundamentally different judgments of the same experience, which do not grow at all merely out of the contemporary social stimuli that have brought them to expression, but spring also from varying cultural heritages which through centuries have

[1] Isa. 4:27 ff.

wrought themselves into the very blood and nerves and tissue of these personalities. Fundamentally, then, the prophets are thinkers, philosophers, men who are striving to hold "a conversation with the whole of the world in which they live," men whose intellectual activities constitute the controlling factor in their psychology, and whose intellectual pre-eminence can only be appreciated, not from the vantage point of the culture of a later age and of another place, but from that of the culture which was dominant when and where they lived.

The philosophical values of the prophetic theology are best appreciated in the light of contemporary modes of thinking about the nature of the world. Since that world expressed its philosophy through the theological symbols it employed in the myths and rituals of the cultus and in the folk tales which often carried the same motifs, one arrives at the world-view through the current conceptions of the gods. As one reads the Old Testament in search of these one discovers that they resolve themselves into three fundamental propositions: (1) The gods are many; (2) the gods are subject to certain controls which can be exerted upon them by, and on behalf of, man; (3) the super-power by virtue of which such controls exist is of a non-personal category, a category other than that in which either gods or men may be placed.

That for the average Israelite, of whatever social class, the gods were many and not one is susceptible of proof, not only from the text of the Old Testament itself, but from the fact that the excavations of various Palestinian sites yield indubitable evidence in substantiation of the text. When, for example, the results of Professor Badè's excavations at Mizpeh are published it will appear that well down into the monarchical period there was a large mother-goddess shrine within a stone's throw of the shrine of Yahweh.

When one follows archaeology one sees more readily the significance of a passage like I Sam. 26:1 ff. wherein the great Judean historian reveals the fact that David himself believed that Yahweh's influence did not extend beyond the borders of Israel. One appreciates, too, the value of such a passage as Judges 2:6-19 for the history of culture. This passage comes from the hand of a later writer who is using earlier material to support the thesis that loyalty to one God is the basis of political safety and who, in doing so, does not hesitate to affirm that such an attitude has not, on the whole, been characteristic of the people of Israel in the past. As a recorder of individual political facts this writer is not trustworthy. But his unreliability in the sphere of individual fact is due to the circumstance that his interest concentrates itself, not on these, but on dominant cultural trends. And in this sphere there is every reason to believe that he is eminently sound when he represents the great majority as stubbornly persisting in polytheism.

Similarly archaeology helps to make concrete the situation reflected in a passage which probably comes from the hand of Jeremiah's biographer, Baruch, and which suggests the part played in the religion of the average citizen from early times by the cult of the Queen of Heaven.[2] Indeed the evidence for the dominance of polytheism among the Hebrews from the time of their entry until well down

[2] Jer. 44:16 ff.

into the Persian period is so strong that the point need not be further elaborated upon. What matters is not the bald fact itself but rather its bearing on the world-view of the average contemporary of the prophets.

One does not need to rely upon any modern interpretation of the world-view which underlies polytheism. The prophet Isaiah expounds it for us in the following oracle:

Ha! Assyria, rod of my anger, and staff of my fury!
Against a godless nation I send him,
And against the people of my wrath I charge him,
To spoil them, and to prey on them,
And to trample them down like the mire of the streets.
But not so does he think,
And not so does he plan;

. . . .

For he says,

. . . .

Inasmuch as my hand has reached to the kingdoms of the idols
Whose carved images were more than those of Jerusalem and
     Samaria
Shall I not do to Jerusalem and its images
As I have done to Samaria and its idols?

. . . .

By the strength of my hand have I done it,
And by my wisdom, for I have understanding.

. . . .

Shall an axe boast itself over the man that hews with it,
Or a saw lord itself over the man that plies it?[3]

Here is a prophet's keen analysis of the nature of the world-view which underlies polytheism. For the Assyrian king to whom he refers was as ardent a polytheist as anyone else though he despised the gods of the nations he

[3] Isa. 10:5 ff.

conquered. But Isaiah represents him as really believing that there is no purpose, plan, or wisdom in the world above his own. By his possession of some secret power he is able to subdue the gods. No deity, to his mind, actually enjoys cosmic sovereignty. There is no unity in the whole of his world. For him the world is the scene of conflict between various deities of whom those who do his will are, for the moment, stronger than those who support his rivals.

In the polytheistic stage the greatest of the gods are no more than the immanent helpers of man. Their function is to fulfil man's plans and satisfy his desires. Thus the world-view is anthropocentric. Polytheism has the same basic philosophy as atheistic humanism. Neither sees the world as part of a meaningful universe but only as the setting of man's essentially meaningless struggle for existence. In neither of them does the basic philosophy permit of man's holding "a conversation with the whole of his world," since the ultimate forces are non-personal and inscrutable.

Beside that dominant polytheistic and anthropocentric world-view which prevailed in the times of the prophets one has but to set these words of a very great anonymous prophet of the Middle Persian period:

> For thus says the high and exalted One,
> Who dwells enthroned forever, and whose name is Holy:
> "I dwell enthroned on high, as the Holy One,
> But with him also that is contrite and humble in spirit,
> To regenerate the spirit of the humble
> And to revivify the heart of the contrite."[4]

[4] Isa. 57:15.

In the world-view which underlies this passage the world is definitely a part of a universe that is the scene of the expression of a cosmic aim and plan which transcends the desires and purposes of man but does not abandon man himself. This is a world with the whole of which man may be in co-operation and communion, a world in which the human experience may be seen as meaningful.

One may turn now to consider the idea that was prevalent in the culture into which the prophets were born, that the gods are subject to certain controls. The prophet Micah makes it clear that this was a common way of thinking about gods in a passage which indicates that his contemporaries thought in this way about Yahweh himself.

> "Do not keep on harping," they harp;
> "One should not be harping upon such things;
>   Shame will not overtake us,"
>   Says the house of Jacob.
> "Is the Lord's spirit impatient,
>   Or are such things his deeds?
>   Do not his words mean good to his people, Israel?"[5]

Here there is expressed that conceit of ability to control his own destinies which seems to have developed in man in correspondence with his increasing power over his natural environment. It expresses, in this passage, not a group's growing confidence in the totality of things, but its confidence in its ability to wrest what it wanted from the totality of things. Yahweh, as Micah's interlocutors conceive him, is under control. They do not belong to him. He belongs to them; and he will assist them to real-

[5] Mic. 2:6 f.

ize their desires, regardless of their deserts, regardless of how those desires and the conduct of these his worshipers may clash with any plan which may inhere in the nature of the totality of things.

It is this conceit of control for the realization of human purposes which Amos attacks in his fourth chapter. There he draws attention to the assiduity with which contemporary society cultivates, through the cultus, this conceit of control. Then he proceeds to enumerate facts which it is impossible to account for on any such world-view. Famine, drought, blight, mildew, pestilence—how, asks Amos, can one account for these on any view that men may coerce the world to their own desires? Is it not more reasonable to believe that there is some power in the world which is beyond coercion? And is it not a more valid conclusion that troubles arise rather from human defiance of this power than from the mere lack of sufficient skill in coercing it?

> Can horses run up a cliff?
> Or can one plow the sea with oxen,
> That you turn justice into poison
> And the fruit of justice into wormwood,
> O you who delight in the unreal,
> Who say, "Have we not, by our own strength,
> Gained dominance?"[6]

One can see at once that underlying these current ideas about the nature of the totality of things there is some deep-rooted feeling from which this conviction has sprung. The root of the matter is not just man's self-sufficiency, as the prophets often suggest. It must go deeper than

[6] Amos 6:12 f.

that else why would man's imagination ever have peopled his world with those superhuman auxiliaries he calls gods? So far as man himself is concerned his basic trouble has not arisen from a native superiority complex but from the reverse. It goes back to that period of his racial history when the world as a whole seemed other than human, when the highest forces within it emanated from an entirely different category, and when every triumph of his, over the superior bestial beings which surrounded him, seemed to him to have become possible only through some essentially accidental alignment of that remote, impersonal, diffused superforce upon his side. From that primitive idea developed magic and taboo. Magic is the art of using that impersonal superforce for human ends. The claims of those who use it grow in direct ratio to man's progress in relating himself successfully to Nature. Taboo really is the technique by which the use of the power is confined to certain channels. Those objects and persons which convey it to the multitude are thought of as being insulated against it to a degree sufficient to make them effective carriers of the power and safe mediators of it to ordinary persons. For one not so immunized it is death to come into direct contact with the power. So Uzzah, an ordinary person, put his hand on Yahweh's ark, wherein such mysterious power resided, and was struck dead in spite of his commendable motives.[7]

Now the immunization of the bearers of this power involves their separation from the category of ordinary humanity and some measure of identification with the category of the superforce itself. The Hebrews called this

[7] II Sam. 6:1 ff.

process sanctification, "the being made holy." In Hebrew the root idea of the word "holy" is "apartness," or "difference in category."

By the days of the great Hebrew prophets the original, primitive, clear-cut ideas about this superforce had already undergone a long process of modification. But the central idea that the superforce is non-personal was very tenacious because of the survival of magic as the cult technique of the dominant pattern. In many religions the high god of the pantheon was thought of as approximating a superforce; but even so he was still conceived of as a capricious, other than genuinely personal, source of power. He was capable, therefore, of inspiring in ordinary men nothing much more than awesome dread.

So long as anything approximating this conception of the superforce had a place in any man's world-view, so long as he believed that the high power in his world was, in some sense, non-personal, or of another category, such a one was thereby rendered incapable of relating himself to the whole of the world because there was that in his world with which he could have no fellowship. Where that pattern of thought held sway it was hard for the average man to conceive any moral order in the universe, hard for him to grasp the idea that human relations could be ultimately based on anything more dependable than physical force.

The prophets all come to grips with that essentially unmoral idea of an impersonal superforce. Amos and Hosea both stress the sovereignty and personality of God, Amos laying the emphasis on the former and Hosea on the latter. But it remained for the great Isaiah to make

most telling use of the terminology of the pattern to re-
fute its philosophy. He does this by insisting that Yahweh *is* the superforce, the Holy One.

> Holy, Holy, Holy is Yahweh of Hosts
> The whole earth is full of his glory.[8]

Since the word here translated "glory" was a term for the
visible manifestation of the deity's power, the meaning of
this formula is "Yahweh is the superforce which manifests itself in the whole of the world." And since, for Isaiah, Yahweh was a highly personal being the import of
this proclamation is that the supreme power, the ultimate reality, is not impersonal but personal.

What a radical idea that was for many of Isaiah's contemporaries is hardly appreciated by a modern world, but
may yet be more appreciated when the same philosophic
battle has to be fought over again. There is one passage,
Isa. 8:11–15, which the prophet uttered in the midst of a
situation in which he had put forth a mighty effort to dis-
credit the cult magic, through reliance upon which his
people were being led into an attitude of fear, when nothing but an attitude of faith, of "dealing in full honor and
trust with the world," might have saved them.

For thus hath Yahweh said to me with inescapable force,
Warning me not to walk in the way of this people:
"Call ye not an alliance what this people calls an alliance!
And its fear fear not ye, nor dread!
Yahweh of hosts, Him regard ye as holy.
Let him be your fear, and him your dread.
For he shall become a holy place, a stone of striking, a rock of
    stumbling to both houses of Israel,
A trap, and a snare, to the ruler of Jerusalem.

[8] Isa. 6:3.

And many shall stumble against them and shall fall,
And they shall be broken and snared and taken."

The difficulties which this passage presents to modern readers are not due to corruption of the text but to failure to appreciate how the language of the prophet was influenced by the language and thought of the society he addressed. That was a society which still clung to magic and in the mind of whose average citizen there still lingered a superstitious dread of mysterious non-personal powers. Perhaps the most puzzling thing in the passage is the impersonal terms with which the prophet identifies Yahweh. He is to be a "holy place," a place where such power manifests itself. He is to be a stone, a rock, a trap, a snare. He, too, is power, can destroy. He, the personal super-force, is more to be feared than whatever awesome, mysterious, impersonal forces seem to lend Assyria its magic might. The supreme reality in the universe is personal; and whoever sets himself in alignment with anti-personal and unmoral forces against that personal and personality-producing power will break himself against the universe itself.

This, then, is the world-view or philosophy of the prophets, that the totality is a universe, all the parts of which are organically related to each other and genetically related to the whole; that the part cannot coerce the whole, but may co-operate with it; and that whatever is anti-personal has no abiding place in a whole which is personal.

CHAPTER V

THE DYNAMIC OF THE PROPHETIC PHILOSOPHY OF LIFE

To modern Western ears it may sound somewhat strange to speak of the specifically intellectual aspects of the prophetic ministry as "the heart of their philosophy of life." Yet the phrase may be justified on two grounds. In the first place it accords with the Hebrew view of the functions of the bodily organs. For they were wont to regard the heart as the seat of the intellect rather than of the emotions, which they were inclined to associate with the abdominal organs. In the second place the phrase may be justified because to Western minds the word "heart" conveys the idea of centrality, since on the dependability of its functioning every part of the whole corporeal structure is dependent.

Whether the Hebrews understood this or not the phrase has here been used with the intent of suggesting the centrality of the intellectual element of the prophetic philosophy of life without divorcing it from those other elements of it which have to do with emotion and will, with feeling and conduct, with desire and action. One wishes, in other words, to emphasize the intellectuality of the prophets without, at the same time, making intellectuals out of them.

It seems desirable, in a complex civilization such as that which here and now prevails, to emphasize the fact that these great religious leaders of Israel achieved intellectual leadership, not in spite of equally well-developed capacities for emotion and action, but because of them. Their thinking has left its mark on humanity because it was organically related to a dynamic drive of desire, on the one hand, and to an undeniable necessity of social expression, on the other. Hence the prophet concerned himself not only with contemporary patterns of thought, but also with the social mood and the social mode.

The significance of the preoccupation of the prophets with the emotional aspects of the dominant culture, of their insistent recurrence to the nature and range of the average man's desires, is appreciated only when one remembers that desire is the dynamic of all life, and when, remembering this, one places the prophets in the midst of a society which was steadily declining in significance, sets them in the midst of a culture which yearly became more inadequate to cope with the pressures and tensions which were inherent in the world-situation.

The prophets appear to have sensed a certain enfeeblement of the dynamic which underlay the currently accepted world-view. They found this *malaise* to be actively or incipiently present throughout all the social groups of the civilized world. Materially successful societies were no more immune from it than were the economic and political casualties in the roll call of nations. Their diagnosis of the cause of the disorder is worthy of some consideration since they found the dominant religion of their day to be deeply involved in it.

As one explores, from the writings of the prophets, the range of desire which dominated the average citizen of all classes one finds it very largely confined to the level of things, to the material products which can be wrung from the soil, the sea, the mine. The words which lingered longest upon the lips of the everyday man, the words which carried the most satisfying savor to his soul, were such words as milk, honey, oil, incense, wine, bread, and a hundred other names for prized and precious things which meant to him the satisfaction of the physical appetites and the egoistic instincts.

> O daughters of Israel, weep over Saul!
> Who clothed you in scarlet daintily,
> Who adorned your garments with gold and jewels.[1]

So sang David of the fallen Saul what was to that age high praise. But long afterward a herald of redemption, whose scale of values had been extended to the realm of the intangible things of the spirit, could only express them through the tangible symbols of the physical satisfactions which had for ages been the chief values in his society. He came to give his people

> a *crown* instead of *ashes*
> The *oil* of joy instead of a *garment* of mourning.[2]

This close association between the physical and the spiritual satisfactions, this sense of the intimate dependence of the one upon the other, this refusal to compartmentalize life, to abstract the spiritual from its setting in the corporeal, to set it apart as something to admire but not to desire, is one of the secrets of the vitality of Hebrew religion. It never loses the drive of desire because it has learned to educate, discipline, and enlarge desire and has not sought merely to suppress it. The stimulus which gave it this capacity it owes in large part to the prophets.

[1] II Sam. 1:24.   [2] Isa. 61:3.

When they appeared upon the scene the dynamic of
the dominant culture was already beginning to fail. A
study of the use by the prophets of the words which convey the idea of growing tired and weary is very revealing.
On a certain occasion in which the validity of the official
cultus was an issue very much at stake Isaiah addressed
the court of Ahaz thus:

> Hear now, O house of David!
> Is it too slight a thing for you to weary men,
> That you must weary my God also?[3]

The prophet feels the futility of the world's way which his
people, under their messianic king, are following. The
same sense of the decline of driving power in the dominant
pattern is reflected by Habakkuk as he surveys not only
the life of his own people but that of the world in which
they are so intimately involved:

> Woe to him who builds a city by bloodshed
> And establishes a town by wrong.
> Are not these things from Yahweh of Hosts
> That peoples exhaust themselves for the fire,
> And nations wear themselves out for naught?[4]

Perhaps the best picture of a worn-out nation is that giv-
en of Babylonia by the great anonymous prophet of the exile. It is doubly significant because it shows how great a
part the religion of that country was playing in the enfeeblement of the dynamic of its life. When one remembers that the Babylonian cultus was but a most elaborate
version of the kind of cultus which had prevailed all over
the Near East for centuries, one understands even better
what Isaiah and Habakkuk mean.

[3] Isa. 7:13.   [4] Heb. 2:12 f.

Your wisdom and skill have led you astray,
So that you said to yourself, "I am and there is none but me."
Therefore disaster shall come upon you
Which you shall not know how to charm away;
And destruction shall fall upon you
Which you shall not be able to appease;
And ruin shall swoop upon you
Which you shall not know how to avert.
Stand, then, by your enchantments, and your many spells,
With which you have wearied yourselves from your youth;
Perhaps you may yet avail, perhaps you may strike terror!
You have wearied yourself with your many counsellors,
Now let them stand and save you—
Those who map out the heavens and gaze at the stars
And tell you month by month what fortune will come to you.
Lo they have become like stubble, the fire burns them,
They cannot save themselves from the power of the flame;
For it is no glowing coal to warm oneself at, no fire to sit before.
Such is the fate of those with whom you have wearied yourself
With whom you have trafficked from your youth—
They stagger each his own way, with none to save them.[5]

Here is an effete and tired nation whose philosophy of life
has lost its dynamic, the sacred custodians of whose culture have used it to exploit its people, and in the process
have lost the gift of vitalizing human spirits, of keeping
alive in the group, as a group, the power and the very desire to survive the social pressures which play upon it.

It is not hard to see how the accepted religion of that
world became involved in a process which had such unfor-
tunate results. All culture is based on the production of
material wealth, on the capacity to create surpluses which
permit diversification of labor and diffusion of its products. Material productivity is the first and most obvious

[5] Isa 47:10 ff.

need of man. He cannot transcend the physical except by attention to the physical. The primitive agricultural religion, therefore, ritualized the basic human actions by which fertility was stimulated and productivity assured. Plowing, cultivating, sowing, reaping, procreation, all acquired sacred sanctions. The system went beyond that and endeavored to regulate and control the part that nature itself played in this co-operative productive process. All the commonly accepted religions of this world were religions of productivity.

It was on the side of the distribution of its products that the system fell down. It is a fact, as everyone knows, that some centralization of material wealth is essential to the most efficient distribution and the most secure enjoyment of it. The true end of this centralization, however, is the ultimate redistribution. But the economic machinery of society cannot function in that way where the material goods which constitute wealth are looked upon as in themselves supremely valuable.

That, however, was the blind alley into which that culture turned under myopic leaders who saw the goods which gave them power to lead, but not the people whose endurance, industry, and skill produced the goods. Such could not but be the case in an anthropocentric and geocentric culture where the purpose of the part, instead of the whole, is dominant. The result was that the controlling elements of society developed a very pretty technique of exploitation which was so effectively buttressed by religious sanctions that it commended itself not only to the exploiter but to the exploited. The basis of it was an emphasis upon the satisfaction of the appetites and the ego.

The shrines became centers of a fellowship based upon these satisfactions in exchange for which the people were led to part with more and more of their wealth to the ruling caste, at the head of which stood the king, who was both secular and religious head of the state. The system worked well enough until the rise of the great struggle for imperial power placed too great demands upon it, until the residue of sustenance which remained for the producer of the wealth was so meager as to undermine his health and sap his spirit. Thus two tendencies went steadily forward under the sanction of the dominant religion. The physique of the race was being undermined by slavish toil and brutish indulgence. The spirits of individuals were being broken and cowed into servility.

One must not forget that this sensual mood of Israelite society, this overemphasis upon the values of physical desire through which the average citizen gradually lost the power to satisfy legitimately many of these desires, was an all but universal mood. It is true that the prophets championed the poor and the oppressed, that they opposed the kings and denounced the upper classes. But one should not forget that the basic trouble here was not class conflict, nor should one make of the prophets champions of such. They were the champions of no class, but rather of a culture which looked toward the mitigation and even the elimination of such conflicts. It was not hidden from them that the money changers who trafficked in personality in the gates and shrines of Israel's cities were there, not merely by virtue of their own shrewdness, but by virtue of the ignorance, inertia, and personal insignificance of the average citizen.

The evidence upon which this picture of the process by which the dynamic of desire was cabined and confined, until membership in that society became no longer a motive widespread and potent enough to lend cohesiveness to the existing order, stands out on nearly every page of the prophetic writings. Amos alludes to the lure and the demoralizing effects of this exaltation of physical values when he says:

For three transgressions of Israel
And for four, I will no more restore it to prosperity
Because they have sold the innocent for silver,
And the needy for the sake of a pair of shoes.
And they buffet the heads of the poor,
And they turn the humble from the way
A man and his father resort to the same harlot
With the result that they profane the nature of my holiness.
Upon garments taken from the exploited they stretch themselves
    beside every altar
And the wine of the duped they drink *in the shrines of their gods.*[6]

Hosea bears witness both to the part played by the dominant religion in fostering this sensual mood, to the diffusion thereof among all classes of society, and to its effect on the solidarity of the family:

Wine and new wine *take away the understanding*
My people inquire of their wood
And their staff instructs them.
For a harlotrous spirit has led them astray,
And they have become apostates from their God.

. . . .

Therefore your daughters play the harlot,
And your sons' wives commit adultery.
I will not punish your daughters when they play the harlot,

[6] Amos 2:6 ff.

Nor your sons' wives when they commit adultery;
For they themselves go apart with harlots
And sacrifice with shrine-prostitutes,
And a people *without insight* must come to ruin.[7]

Here, too, it is clear that Hosea is aware of the relation
between this dominant social mood and the philosophical
inadequacy of the pattern. These are people whose emotional life has got out of hand because their view of the
world fosters that way of feeling.

Jeremiah wistfully voices his conviction that the whole
social mood must be changed and specifically points out
not only the loss of emotional values, but the decline of
economic strength which has accompanied that indulgence of the mood which the prevailing religion has coun-
tenanced:

See! we come to thee;
For thou art the Lord our God.
Truly, in vain is the clamor from the hills.
Truly, in the Lord our God rests the security of Israel.
From our youth has the shameful thing devoured the fruits of our
    fathers' toil,
Their flocks and their herds, their sons and their daughters;
So let us lie down in our shame, and let our dishonor enfold us,
For against the Lord our God have we sinned, both we and our
    fathers,
From our youth until now.[8]

The prophets were able to contribute to the revitaliza-
tion of the society into which they were born because they
developed a capacity for enlarging and disciplining the
waning drive of desire. They added to the things for
which it was worthwhile for their group to go on striving

---

[7] Hos. 4:11 ff.   [8] Jer. 3:22 ff.

to perpetuate its life as a group. They did something to the current range of values; and after they did what they did the dominant pattern of culture was never quite the same as it had been before.

One does not desire to leave the impression that they thought of what they were doing as an effort to enrich and ennoble contemporary conceptions of value. Had that been the case one could find more specific statements of such an aim in their writings. As it is one has to deduce any positive statement of their contributions at this point largely from their negative criticisms of the accepted scale of values.

One would like to make the point that the prophets were not ascetics. As a rule, though they are sometimes otherwise represented, they did not seek the solution of the problem by any confinement of the productive activities of their people. Their insight was not that the satisfaction of the physical is, in itself, wrong but that such satisfactions are never adequate to the whole human need.

What sometimes makes the prophets appear to be ascetics is not their concern with productivity but with acquisitiveness. Many of them had not a little contempt for the mere refinements and adornments of life. Isaiah rails at the fashionably dressed ladies of Jerusalem, and has no more use for the amassing of precious metals, horses, chariots, and all the other accoutrements of those who followed the world's way than he has for idols.[9] But this is not asceticism. It does not spring from any idea that desire is to be stifled. It rises from his concern over the basic problem of distribution. Isaiah here is really

[9] Isa. 2:7 f.; 3:16 ff.

thinking about the content of the heap of things that constitute the wealth of his country, which, as anyone knows, is fully as important as its mere volume. Solomon poured a flood of the products of the toil of his peasantry onto the markets of Tyre in exchange for the cedars and metals and craftsmanship which went into the building of the temple.[10] The temple did much, no doubt, to adorn and beautify his capital and to enrich the life of his people. But the issue which was raised at his death, and which cost his successor the greater half of his kingdom, was whether the acquisitive individual is justified in diverting the basic products which sustain life to other uses so long as there are those who produce them whose life is not adequately sustained.[11]

In the very nature of the case trafficking in the goods which are basic to the sustenance of life is trafficking in life itself. Only actual surpluses of such things over and above adequate satisfaction of human need may be legitimately diverted to other uses.

The economic maladjustments which stimulated the prophets to protest against the system which rationalized and fostered them were due to the misuse of over-centralized wealth. But what concerned them more than the damage to men's bodies was the damage to their spirits. The words which they used in connection with these concrete economic and social situations, words such as *justice, kindness, righteousness, honor, trust, faithfulness, decency,* and so on, are words which signify spiritual relationships which arise from the disciplining of the desire

[10] I Kings 5:1 ff.   [11] I Kings 12:4 ff.

for material things. In a world devoted to production the prophets arose to speak of distribution, not for the inherent values of the things which were to be distributed, but for the spiritual values which would accrue to society through their distribution. They were men who had come to see that ('man does not live by bread alone,"[12] that he is man because his desire is both capable of discipline and of unlimited enlargement.

[12] Deut. 8:3; cf. Matt. 4:4; Luke 4:4.

CHAPTER VI

THE EXPRESSION OF THE PROPHETIC PHILOSOPHY OF LIFE

It has already been suggested that the thinking of the prophets was not only related to a dynamic drive of enlarging desire, on the one hand, but also, on the other, to an undeniable necessity of social expression. There are those who fail to appreciate the prophets as men of action because they seldom displayed any organizing ability, any gift for creating institutions designed to express their own philosophy. To such the prophet appears to be, executively speaking, a futile person, and, in the short view, there is some justification for this judgment. The individual prophet often lives his life like Shelley's "luminous angel beating his wings in a void."

But the long view yields one quite a different picture of Israel's prophets. For on such a view it becomes clear that in the foreground of the picture, at the moment when Israel makes the transition from one stage of its cultural evolution to another, stands one or more of these champions of cultural advance, not in the self-seeking attitude of those who would personally profit through crisis, but as those who carry the hope of the unborn generations in their mind. It was, one must believe, so far as the nature of his personality is concerned, a prophet who led certain Hebrew tribesmen from slavery in the midst of plenty through a trying discipline in the niggardly desert and pointed them to the scene of a more abundant life, participation in which was denied to him. It was a prophet, impressed by the inadequacy of patriarchal tribalism, who initiated the movement by which a monarchy was established. It was a prophet who, when that way of life proved inadequate, seized the moment to point his people to another method of integrating their life and conserving their culture.[1]

The very attitude of the prophets to institutions, their conception of the social function of institutions, is such as to hold them back from putting their faith in them, or from thinking that man can change himself by conducting the business of living through some different institutional structure. To the prophets, with their profound sense of cosmic purpose, with their deep-seated faith in man's capacity to discover new values in life, the function of the institution was not to regiment life but to liberate it and to fulfil its promise. To them this mighty ongoing stream of life was itself the reality; and they seem to have been characterized by a certain restraint toward the established institutional order which rises, not from executive incapacity, but from the sense that the stream of life is stronger than the dikes men build to hold it. For them it is life which molds institutions rather than institutions that mold life. So their criticism is directed at life as it functions in institutions, at the personnel of the institution rather than at the institution as such.

In the days of the prophets the institutional framework of society no longer sufficed for the needs of life in an imperialistic world. Powerless to rouse the flagging personal forces of the people, the average institutionalist

[1] Moses, Samuel, and Ezekiel.

lent himself, consciously or unconsciously, to the mere regimentation and exploitation of his fellows, striving to retain some shred of significance for himself at the cost of the insignificance of the group of which he was a part.

The prophetic attitude to institutions comes out in their relationships with the contemporary kings. The prophets are highly critical of most kings, not as kings, but as persons. The significance of this point only becomes clear when it is understood that Israel's kings claimed to be something more than just persons. They claimed to be, in some sense, divine persons. David was the first Israelite, so far as one knows, to conform to the pattern which had long been accepted among more highly civilized nations in this matter of the messianic sacrosanctity of the holder of the kingly office. When the headstrong Abishai wished to pin Saul to the earth with his spear, David's refusal to allow this was explained thus to the zealous youth:

As Yahweh lives, either Yahweh shall smite him, or his day shall come to die, or he shall go down into the battle and perish, Yahweh forbid that I should put forth my hand against Yahweh's Messiah.[2]

By virtue of his office the person of Saul is sacrosanct. He is the seal on Yahweh's right hand, the incarnation of the deity's purpose for Israel. He is above the law. His will is the will of God.

It cost a hard struggle at first to impose this conception of the kingship upon the then high-spirited Hebrew clansmen. It has been recently suggested in conversation[3] that

[2] I Sam. 26:10 f.

[3] By the writer's friend and student, Mrs. Ross Rogers.

this may have been the issue between the party which supported Solomon and the group which threw in their lot with Adonijah. The latter's bid for the office was through the suffrage of sympathetic leaders of the state.[4] But Solomon is anointed by a priest and rides to the ceremony on the mule of King David.[5] His coronation, in other words, corresponds to a pattern which had been conventional in the settled lands from time immemorial, while Adonijah is proclaimed as the Bedouins proclaim a leader.

Solomon's career follows, in every respect, the pattern of the kings of the civilized world. He is the autocratic vicegerent of God, who is above the law, subject only to whatever he may believe, or be led to believe, is the will of God. That ancient pattern gradually intrenches itself in both Hebrew kingdoms after the disruption. But throughout the centuries the great nonconformist prophets maintain an irreconcilable attitude to it. They never accept the dogma that the will of the king is *ipso facto* the will of the god. They insist that the king is king by virtue of no ceremonial magic but only by virtue of his ability to function, in actual social relationships, as the conserver of the nation's life. Whenever they do not so qualify, the prophets unhesitatingly denounce them. They judge the king by his contribution to the common weal.

So Micaiah ben Imlah will predict only defeat for Ahab who is ready to plunge his people into war to gratify his personal ambitions.[6] So Hosea does not hesitate to announce the downfall of the house of Jehu,[7] because the

---

[4] I Kings 1:24 ff.   [6] I Kings 22:2 ff.

[5] I Kings 1:33 f.   [7] Hos. 1:4 ff.

performances of its monarchs have impoverished and cor-
rupted Israel. So Isaiah scorns the messianic pretensions
of Ahaz, holding the cultus ritual through which the
king's status as messiah is yearly dramatized for the
benefit of the people up to ridicule, because this king is
impotent to conserve the significance of the state and
therefore unable to function as the enricher of the satisfactions of his people.[8]

On the same grounds the prophets attack the way persons function through other institutions. When Amos
says:

> Come to Bethel, and—transgress!
> In Gilgal multiply your transgressions!
> Bring your sacrifices every morning,
> And every three days your tithes.
> Burn a thank offering of leavened bread,
> And proclaim free-will-offerings; publish them
> For so you love to do, O Israelites.[9]

he is not attacking sacrifice as an institution but the conduct of the average worshiper which divorces the institution from any real relationship to the social weal.

Micah finds that the personnel of the institutions of
his day is hindering instead of promoting the average
citizen from co-operating with God, from relating himself
to reality.

> Thus has the Lord said,
> Regarding the prophets who lead my people astray,
> Who preach prosperity when their mouth is filled;
> But if one does not put something in their mouths,
> They declare war against him!
> Therefore it shall be night for you, without vision,

[8] Isa. chap. 7.   [9] Amos 4:4 f.

And darkness for you without divination
For the sun shall set upon the prophets,
And the day shall become dark over them

. . . .

Her chiefs pronounce judgment for a bribe,
And her priests declare oracles for hire,
And her prophets divine for cash.
Yet they lean upon the Lord, saying,
"Is not the Lord in the midst of us?
No misfortune can befall us."[10]

The allusion here to the same ritual which Isaiah repudiates in his Immanuel oracle seems to one who studies the underlying pattern of the dominant cultus quite obvious. Through the Immanuel (God-with-us) symbol there may be inculcated an anthropocentric world-view which makes the deity subservient to his worshipers. This philosophy has not a little to do with the divorcing of the institutions of the time from any proper social function. Through them men function anti-socially. The institutions do not liberate men to a more abundant life through relating them to a social purpose.

The part which magic played in the subversion of institutions to anti-social uses was very great. Magic, as has been pointed out, has its roots in the accepted view of the world with its conceit of control of nature by an impersonal superforce, through mysteries known only to the holy initiate. Through the last several years archaeology and exegetical research have been slowly forcing students of Hebrew culture to see that the cult technique of the popular religion, even down into late times, was preponderantly magical.

[10] Mic. 3:15 f., 11.

Wherever such a condition obtains it is inevitable that a tendency should arise to make the conduct pattern static through elaborate institutionalization. This is so because the ethic of a religion which employs a magical technique is almost wholly ceremonial, and because the ceremonial becomes a vested interest for those who are qualified to administer it.

The classic statement of the prophetic position on that point occurs in Mic. 6:6 ff.

> Wherewith shall I come before the Lord,
> And bow myself before God most high?
> Shall I come before him with burnt-offerings,
> With calves a year old?
> Will the Lord be placated with thousands of rams,
> With myriads of streams of oil?
> Shall I give my first born for my transgression,
> The fruit of my body for the sin of my soul?
> You have been told, O man, what is good:
> Yet what does the Lord require of you,
> But to do justice and to love kindness
> And to walk humbly with your God?[11]

According to this passage the ethic is not absolute, but the social principle of fellowship with men, and with the universe as a whole, is absolute. The true philosophy cannot be expressed in any static ethic rigidly set in institutional forms.

That makes the prophetic attitude to institutions as such perfectly clear and helps one to understand why it is touched with indifference. To them no institution is worth preserving, in any particular form, for its own sake. The value of any institution is in direct ratio to its adapta-

[11] Cf. Amos 5:21 ff.; Isa. 58:5 ff.

bility to the changing conditions under which valid and growing human needs, needs which fall within the category of fellowship, are to be met. What matters most is not the structure or form of the institution but the spirit with which it is suffused, the fundamental attitude to life, of those who function socially through it.

That, perhaps, is why the prophets hold an evolutionary rather than a revolutionary attitude to institutions. The on-going personality-producing process will sooner or later cast into the discard all institutions which do not harmonize with the purpose that informs this personal universe. That is why the prophets criticize existing institutions, but only step in to set up new ones when the old ones, through the dry rot superinduced in them by those who do not comprehend the function of institutions, have fallen into hopeless disintegration.

The prophets live in the hearts of men and their souls go marching gallantly on precisely because of this insight which saves them from becoming shallow and conceited programmatists. For those who know, the prophets interpret this charming vagueness of theirs about institutions, and this intense preoccupation of theirs with persons and personal relationships, as evidence of a most refreshing sense of human worth and a most comforting faith in the sovereignty of God. To come within the sweep of their spirit is to enter a world where men live, where personality survives the discipline of living to become mellow and radiant and free and victorious.

CONCLUSION

CHAPTER VII

THE PROPHETS AND PROGRESS

It has been remarked by a modern prophet that "progress" is a term which designates a myth that took its rise from the sentimentality of the Victorian era. There is, perhaps, a sense in which this is true. Those who lived in that age saw much of the quick and easy return of profit which accompanies a period of great technological advance. At the time, too, the new science was in the first flush of an almost limitless self-confidence. In that world it took the place that cult magic had held in the world of the ancients. It was the technique of human control over superhuman forces, the new method of coercing or subjugating nature. Before its assault the old world-views crumbled because the religious systems which held them were inadequate for the needs of a swiftly changing order.

That inadequacy was due in part to the fact that few of those systems had conserved the pure prophetic philosophy of life. In fact they had received it, in the first place, only in a much diluted form, through a culture pattern which had drawn much more heavily upon the philosophy the prophets had opposed than upon the prophetic philosophy itself. The Victorian age, therefore, in spite of its Ruskins and Carlyles, found it easy to develop a myth of progress, a sentimental hope that the new magic would save the world, that the startling advance on the technological side of life would itself solve the moral and spiritual problems which the human race might confront.

The Victorian age did, perhaps, develop a myth of progress. But that does not at all mean that progress is a myth, in the sense of that term as employed by those who do not understand the part myth has played in human life. It only means, in the light of all that has happened to the world since those coy and credulous days, that progress is not genetically related to technological ingenuity. It only means that mere cleverness about things is as capricious, so far as its social effects are concerned, as any ancient deity, and may just as easily lead to destruction as to security and happiness.

But that is no new insight, save only to those whose researches into the meaning of human history carry them no farther back than the dawn of the age of the new science and the rise of the machine to dominance over man. Long ago the prophets of Israel had become as completely disillusioned about the futility of mere technological advance as the most rebellious modern radical. They had learned well the lesson that the ground of faith in progress never lies in the external and tangible symbols of human cleverness. Israel may be dotted with houses of hewn stone which completely outmode the camel-hair tent or rude mud hut of an earlier age; her palaces may be furnished with new-fangled ivory-inlaid furniture, and with richly woven cloths of Damascus—but Amos finds no comfort in that. The cunningly wrought idols of gold and silver which adorn the up-to-date sanctuaries of Israel fill Hosea with no hope for a decadent nation. The organizing genius of big business does not suffice to impress Isaiah with any confidence of human progress:

> Perished are the people of the coast land,
>> The merchants of Zidon,
> Who traversed the sea, whose business lay
>> On many waters,
> Whose harvest was grain from the Nile
> Whose revenue was trade with the nations.[1]

The magic skills of the husbandman, far advanced as
they were over the crude techniques of Stone Age days,
give Jeremiah no sense of human progress, bumper though
the crop may be:

> Hark the salvation cry of the daughter of my people
>> Far and wide through the land;
> "Is the Lord not in Zion?
> Is not her king in her midst?"
> "Yes! But why have they vexed me with their images,
>> With their pagan vanities?"—
> The harvest is past, the summer is over,
>> And we are not saved.[2]

So it was with all the prophets. Technological triumph
never inspired them with hope of human advance. Mere
multiplication of things made them despondent. For
them, as Gilbert Murray says, "Progress did not depend
on discoveries and material advances which can be ac-
cumulated and added up."

In so far as those who today decry the concept of progress mean to throw a dash of cold water on humanity's
fast-dwindling conceit over its technological cleverness,
one has no quarrel with them. A generation which has
wiped out literally millions of brave spirits with fiendishly
clever weapons, which finds its intricate mechanisms used

[1] Isa. 23:2 f.   [2] Jer. 8:19 f.

to provide immunity for its irresponsibles, may not be too touchy on this subject of its technological skill.

But when it comes to an epigrammatical dismissal of progress as nothing more than a myth of the much abused and little understood Victorian age, that is to say, a mere imaginative conceit (for it is so that some understand myth), then it is clearly time to go more deeply into the matter.

Let it be agreed at the outset that progress is a myth. It is precisely that fact which involves it with religion. For myth has always functioned as a vehicle of philosophy, of human judgments, attitudes, and convictions, about man and the meaning of his life. Even the Victorian age's myth of progress takes on a different aspect when one remembers this. There is something more to it than imaginative conceit, some dim perception of destiny, some, however futile, groping after order and satisfaction, something that is therefore religious.

It is this insight which Gilbert Murray expresses when he writes: "And as to Progress, it is no doubt a real fact. To many of us it is a truth which lies somewhere near the roots of our religion." Precisely so! It lies so near the roots of religion that those who have the religious outlook cannot be supine when progress is casually impugned. There is something at stake here which has to do with the deepest drives of life, something which cannot be settled by argument, by the mere citation of fact and condition, something which is too elusive and intangible to be the subject of demonstration, pro or con. Who can measure the flight of the human spirit through the long ages since conscious life began? Who can assess what has ceaselessly gone on in that span of time, within countless millions of persons?

This question of progress is not one that can be settled by assertion and argument. Long, toilsome, disinterested research into the life of the past and of the present may ultimately illuminate judgment. But for practical purposes the word "progress" denotes, not a demonstrable fact, but an article of faith. It evokes a response rather than a judgment. One must say to it one or the other of those alternatives which Carlyle expressed as the "Everlasting No" and the "Everlasting Yes." One's feeling about progress wells from one's philosophy of life, from one's view of the world, from the range of one's desire, from the quality of one's actions.

It is a fact that one often has to turn to those who are most pessimistic about the contemporary situation to hear at all the ringing note of genuine optimism, the underlying, unquenchable faith in the meaningfulness of the human struggle, which rests upon no contemporary circumstance of prosperity, but upon a sound cultural heritage that conserves long social experience. If one is too much preoccupied with those conditions which caused so many of the prophets to be pessimistic about their own times, if one goes to them only to find verbal brickbats which may be used in what appear to be parallel situations in his own time, one may easily fail to appreciate that underlying optimism which never surrenders to cynicism no matter how cause for doing so may arise like scum to the surface of contemporary life.

The shepherd of Tekoa travels to Bethel not alone to denounce social maladjustment and predict retribution

but also to say: "Seek me, that ye may live."[3] Under-
neath all his certainty that a decadent social order will
collapse like a moth-eaten garment, there is an assurance
that human failure has no part in the divine purpose, that
not collapse and death but fulness of life is the ultimate
intent of the totality of things.

Hosea, blackest of all pessimists about the immediate
issue of the contemporary situation, yet sees all the more
clearly and steadily the deep and eternal purpose of the
divine will to ennoble humanity.

> When Israel was a child, I came to love him,
> And from Egypt I called him.
> The more I called them,
> The more they went away from me;
>
> . . . .
>
> But it was I who taught Ephraim to walk;
> I took them up in my arms;
> But they did not know that I cared for them.[4]

As Hosea sees the world, progress is one of its deepest
realities. That man should walk and not faint, that he
should grow into fulness of life and not sink into failure
and extinction, inheres in the nature of the universe. That
profound conviction is what makes Hosea's pessimism
about those who have defied that purpose so uncompro-
misingly final.

Habbakuk, after his mind has ranged over the whole
problem of man's inhumanity to man, after he has al-
lowed himself to question the validity of his heritage of
prophetic philosophy, concludes that such things as he
has seen need not be, that it is not in the nature of things
that humanity should not make progress:

[3] Amos 5:4.   [4] Hos. 11:1 ff.

I will take my stand upon my watch tower,
And station myself upon the rampart;
And watch to see what he will say to me,
And what answer he will make to my complaint.
Then the Lord answered me, saying,
"Write the vision clearly upon the tablets,
That one may read it on the run.
For the vision is a witness for the appointed time,
And speaks of the end, and does not lie.
If it tarry wait for it;
For it will surely come without delay.
Verily, the wicked man—I take no pleasure in him;
But the righteous lives by reason of his integrity.
How much less shall the exploiter live
The arrogant worldling, who is without kindliness,
Who enlarges his capacity like Sheol
And is as insatiable as death."[5]

In the last line of this passage there is a very pretty allusion to current mythology. Death, the Hebrew word for which is now read as *mâ-weth* is personalized in the Ras Shamra rituals as *Môt*. It is quite possible that as Habakkuk spoke this passage he said:

Who enlarges his capacity like Sheol
And is as insatiable as Môt.

When one remembers that this oracle was directed against a contemporary divine emperor who claimed to be the incarnation, not of the god of Death, but of the god of Life, the irony of the prophet takes on a sharper edge. Humanity, he feels certain, can and must throw off the shackles of these untrustworthy ones who suffer from the deep-seated malady of fear, from a sense that the whole is inscrutable, not to be dealt with "in full honor and trust,"

[5] Hab. 2:1 ff.

and who therefore feel as Professor Hocking puts it that "their only possible policy is one of struggling with might and main to gain for themselves by snatching from the whole what they can."

Likewise Jeremiah smarting under the misunderstanding and persecution of his contemporaries is tempted again and again to deal with the world in the world's way, tempted to yield to cynicism to give up his faith in the meaningfulness of life, tempted to conceive his Yahweh as one who could also yield with him to the desire for vengeance, to the brute instinct to fight back against a cruel world, tempted, that is, to take the view that the ultimate reality in the universe is non-personal force. But he cannot do it. All that he suffers cannot drive him to do it. There is that inhering in and through the whole which calls him back to the faith, back to the torn and tattered standard of progress.

So Jeremiah cries to Yahweh from the bitterness of this mood, from the edge of the yawning chasm of the "Everlasting No":

> Thou must be in the right, O Lord,
> If I take issue with thee:
> Yet would I lay my case before thee:
> Why does the way of the wicked prosper?
> Why do all the exploiters revel in ease?
> Thou plantest them, and they take root;
> Near art thou in their mouths,
> But far from the desires that drive them.
> Yet thou, O Lord, knowest me,
> Thou seest me, and testest my mind toward thee.
> Pull them out like sheep for the shambles,
> And devote them to the day of slaughter!
> How long must the land mourn.

> And all the herbs of the field wither?
> Through the wickedness of those who dwell in it
> Bird and beast are swept away;
> For they say "God is blind to our ways."[6]

But there is better stuff than that in Jeremiah. He cannot bring himself to harbor in that chaotic whirlpool of cynicism. There is that in the whole of his world which says to him that that is the response of a coward:

> If you have raced with men on foot, and they have beaten you,
> How will you compete with horses?
> And if you take to flight in a safe land,
> How will you do in the jungle of Jordan?[7]
> . . . .
> If you turn, I will endow you with power to survive,
> You shall embody reality;
> If you bring forth what is precious, free of false philosophy,
> You shall be my mouthpiece.
> They may turn to you,
> But you shall not turn to them
> And I will make you toward this people
> A fortified wall of bronze;
> They may fight against you.
> But they shall not overcome you;
> For I am with you to help you
> And to deliver you is the oracle of the Lord.[8]

That is just Jeremiah's theological way of expressing his deep conviction that the ultimate reality is personal, that in the end the "personality-producing forces in the universe" must triumph, that progress, in the deepest sense of the word, is in the eternal scheme of things— progress not of the few, but of the race that the few will

---

[6] Jer. 12:1–4.
[7] Jer. 12:5.   [8] Jer. 15:19 ff.

bring to spiritual birth. For Jeremiah, a great religious soul, is here agonizing to bring a culture to birth, to stimulate in it the forces that make for life, to defeat the forces which make for death. Yahweh is holding him to the fulfilment of the truly religious function, for he is demanding of him that he return to the task of imparting significance to Israel's way of life, of trying to make the life of his people fall into meaningful patterns. Israel must develop persons capable of growing in the bonds of fellowship, capable of using the material goods of life for the promotion of the sense of freedom, happiness, and well-being in the hearts of all members of the fellowship.

The prophetic pessimism, then, is optimism in reverse. It never sours into cynicism. It never slips over the brink into defeatism. It rests upon a genuine realism that seeks facts and will not compromise with sham. But it is not the kind of pessimism that feeds on itself. The prophets are not *poseurs*. They are not dramatizing themselves in tragic rôles. They *are* tragedy. They are the nerve-ends which signal to the whole body politic the pains of decay and approaching dissolution.

Carlyle once remarked about Goethe that he "had to write his *Sorrows of Werther* before the spirit freed itself and he could become a man." His mood was the tragic mood of the immature, of those who enjoy tragedy, as the hypochondriac enjoys ill health, often to the point of simulating it. There is not a little pessimism of this lachrymose type abroad today, pessimism that has no deep undergirding of faith, pessimism that ridicules progress with sob-choked voice. It is that type of pessimism which, among other things, has of late years devoted it-

self to an insidious assault upon the democratic ideal, the
pessimism of those who have no faith in man but unlimited confidence in men. They have been very busy telling
the world what a wicked world it is, what a hapless, hopeless clod is the average man, busy laying the ax to the
roots of the tree of humanity's life. It is time that these
histrionic pessimists should give place to others of the
true prophetic type who might become the precursors of
a new age of progress—not technological progress, but
personal progress.

It would seem to be a self-evident proposition that the
condition of such progress must be the freeing of the human spirit. There is a tradition to the effect that Jesus
began his public ministry on the precise understanding
that his mission was to free the human spirit and that he
chose to express it in the words of one of Israel's prophets. The words which are attributed to him on that occasion might be translated from the language of their prophetic author, and with their immediately following context, as follows:

> The spirit of the Lord Yahweh is upon me
> Because Yahweh hath anointed me;
> To hearten the lowly hath he sent me,
> To reintegrate the intellectually confused,
> To decree flight for the restrained.
> And, for the repressed, release of vitality,
> To proclaim Yahweh's year of approval,
> Our God's vindicating day,
> To comfort all mourners,
> To give to them a garland instead of ashes,
> Oil of joy instead of mourning,
> A vestment of praise instead of a heavy spirit.
> To ordain them as the oaks of victory,

> Yahweh's planting for the glorification of himself.
> And they shall build the ancient wastes
> Shall rehabilitate the ruins of the past.[9]

The spirit and meaning of this passage do not fully disclose themselves to those who see the prophet only in the light of political history. It is true that the situation which he desired to mend was precipitated by political disaster. But it is just as true that the great obstacles which stand in the way of the restoration of his people to a significant place in the world are not political but cultural. The rehabilitation of Jerusalem, and of the Jewish community whose life is centered there, is being frustrated, as anyone may see by reading chapters 56–59, not through political interference on the part of foreigners, but through the paralyzing effects of an ancient philosophy of life. Just as of old, under an entirely different form of government, the personal forces of Israel and Judah had not sufficed to withstand defeat, so now the hardly won restoration movement is threatened by a culture, a way of living, which deadens intellectual alertness, which cowes and breaks the spirit of the common people by treating them as though they were of no significance save to do the pleasure of the domineering few.[10]

Such a suppressed, confused, and spiritless people cannot rebuild the ruins of the damaged past, cannot restore the dead Israel to life, cannot rebuild walls of mud and stone, let alone those emotional, mental, and ethical defenses which are requisite to spiritual growth. Clearly this prophet is an apostle of what has come down to the modern world by intricate channels as the democratic

[9] Isa. 61:1 ff.; cf. Luke 4:16.   [10] Cf. Neh. 5.

ideal. His first demand is for the freeing of the human spirit, for the ennobling of the manhood and womanhood of the group. Only the free can grow. Only the liberated can live constructive lives, lives that make for progress, lives that glorify the God who lives in all things.

Relatively speaking, it has, perhaps, been one of the misfortunes of humanity that the word "democracy" was ever invented. It was never a big enough word for the concept it was meant to denote, certainly not big enough for that concept as one distils it out of the spirit of Israel's prophets. It is a word which has a definitely institutional coloring. It fixes attention on a certain method of freeing the human spirit, and has come to mean what Carlyle despised as "ballot-boxing." Carlyle's insight that "ballot-boxing" alone would not do this business for humanity was eminently sound. But that should not deter one from remembering that the concept behind the word "democracy" means vastly more than mere "ballot-boxing." It means the dignity and worth of manhood and womanhood. It means the inalienable right of every individual to be a person—not just an instrument. It implies cooperation not coercion, reasoning not regimentation, in the regulation of social relationships. It requires of its leadership service, not swank, candor not condescension, privation not the assumption of privilege.

But from what, one may ask, is the human spirit to be freed? The older culture patterns which have been crashing about the ears of recent generations had a language of their own for the answering of that question. They said that man had to be saved from sin and from the punishment which awaited the sinner at the hands of a

God who was jealous of his authority. Sin was the individual person's defiance of authority. That was a very ancient conception of sin—rebelliousness under constituted authority. The Assyrian kings in their inscriptions constantly say of politically rebellious vassals, "He sinned against me," that is to say, he missed the mark, he strayed from the path, he defied the order that through the king had been imposed upon mankind.

That whole way of thinking about sin as an individual defiance of an established and dominant order has been having a hard time in the world of late years. But it is only when one studies the word in the light of its cultural setting that one sees why this is so. That idea of sin originated in a culture which regarded physical force as the ultimate reality and which therefore founded its ethic on the dogma that whatever is is right. Sin is individual divergence from a static ethic, an accepted pattern of conduct. It is individual disobedience of the dictates of the powers that be which, because they be, are ordained of God. Under such a view the spirit of man is only freed by submission to the powers that be, to the standards and patterns that dominate the group, that is to say, by acquiescence in the *status quo*. The free man is a "Yes Man."

It is interesting to contrast with this view of freedom what Gilbert Murray has to say on the subject.

What one always needs for freedom is some sort of escape from the thing that now holds him. A man who is the slave of theories must get outside them and see facts; a man who is the slave of his own desires and prejudices must widen the range of his experience and imagination. But the thing that enslaves us most, narrows the

range of our thought, cramps our capacities and lowers our standards, is the mere Present—the present that is all around us, accepted and taken for granted, as we in London accept the grit in
the air and the dirt on our hands and faces. The material present,
the thing that is omnipotent over us, not because it is either good or
evil, but just because it happens to be here, is the great Jailer and
Imprisoner of Man's mind. . . . . It is not the conventions of the
seventeenth or eighteenth century that now make men conventional. It is the conventions of our own age.[11]

One may suppose that the author of these words
gleaned this insight from his long and profound studies of
the cultural history of the Greeks and, in particular, from
the writings of their philosophers. But the truth which
is here expressed is just as clearly suggested to one who
studies the prophets and Israel's culture. (When the
prophets are placed against the background of the culture that dominated Israel in their times, then the whole
impact of the movement launches itself against any dogma of mere acquiescence in the *status quo*, any submissive-
ness under an assumption that the powers that be in human society are *ipso facto* ordained of God. The "Yes
Man" is not a saint. He is a sinner, or in any case a potential sinner. He is not free, no matter how much ease of
body or mind he enjoys. He is a slave. A slave to what
now is, who only escapes from what now is by submitting
to whatever else may come to be, never by giving himself
to something that ought to be, to something that free
spirits might help to bring to pass.

This revision of the doctrine of sin which has been going on in theological circles in recent years and which has

[11] G. Murray I, *Tradition and Progress*. (Boston–New York: Mifflin,
1922), p. 19.

shifted so much of the responsibility for violation of the established order from the individual to society has, then, much to warrant it in the teaching and example of Israel's prophets. They, too, felt that men could fall into sin, could lose the freedom of their spirits, by conforming to what was regarded in the dominant pattern as righteous, as the will of God. They, too, were disposed to lay upon society much of the blame for the individual's bondage to an evil way of life.

But that is not the whole of the story, and it is the failure to stress the remainder of it which disquiets many people with this new emphasis on society's responsibility for the sins of the individual. The prophets did believe with all their souls that the dominant culture pattern of Israel was responsible for much degradation of individual persons. But they also believed, with equal intensity, that the individual was responsible for the dominant pattern, that society was as it was because individuals bartered their freedom to make it what it ought to be, in exchange for a mess of pottage, in exchange for the fleeting satisfactions of appetite, in exchange for the delusion that their problems could be solved without any co-operation on their part in the understanding of the nature of those problems, and in the development of ways and means of meeting them.

This note of the individual's responsibility for the culture by which he lives is struck by Isaiah in the chapter where he relates the experience by which he himself was summoned to bear his share of it. Immediately upon his own response "Here am I! send me" he hears Yahweh speaking in ironical tones these words:

> Go and say to this people:
> "Keep on hearing, without discerning;
> Keep on seeing, without perceiving."
> Make the *mind* of this people gross,
> Dull their ears, and besmear their eyes;
> Lest they see with their eyes, and hear with their ears,
> *And have a mind to understand, and turn, and be healed.*[12]

Hosea likewise holds the people who accept the culture and the personnel of the cultus who are its custodians responsible for the failure to free themselves from it:

> Yet let no one make charges, and let no one accuse;
> For with you is my quarrel, O priest:
> And you shall stumble by day,
> The prophet also shall stumble with you by night
> And I will destroy your people.
> My people are destroyed *for want of knowledge*—
> Because you have rejected knowledge
> I will reject you from being my priest
>
> . . . .
> They feed on the sin of my people,

(And here sin is certainly not defiance of the powers that be but compliance with them!)

> And for their guilt they whet their appetite
> So it has become "like people, like priest"
>
> . . . .
> And a people *without insight* must come to ruin.[13]

If one wishes to appreciate the contribution of the prophets to the cultural progress of their people one must not try at all to measure it solely by the success they achieved in bringing their own peculiar philosophy of life to social expression. The prophetic way was, so to speak, a rival culture in the making. And, if one considers it only

[12] Isa. 6:9 f.   [13] Hos. 4:4 ff.

as such, one may say that the prophets were futile, that
their actual effect upon the life of the average citizen was
nil. So considering the prophetic way, many are inclined
to see the prophets as men who talked much but achieved
nothing, because they were always dealing with the intangible things of the spirit and never grappled with the
business of doing anything about the more practical realities of life, except, perhaps, in a few cases where prophets
were mixed up in political intrigues which resulted in
dynastic change.

So far as the great prophets who have here been dis-
cussed are concerned, even this claim of having successfully participated in court politics cannot be made for
them. The prophets who do that sort of thing are prophets within the dominant system itself—cult prophets.
Such for example was the individual dispatched by Elisha
to inaugurate the murderous revolt against civilization
which was headed up by Jehu.[14] But the great prophets
are seldom in the system in the sense of functioning
through the regular machinery of government. Not often
do they score any practical successes of that order. They
are not, as a rule, men of consequence in that sense of
the term. Even the great Isaiah's relationships with
Hezekiah fluctuated, and his counsels were not consistent-
ly sought or followed. And, when a crisis was precipitated
in the court of Josiah by the finding of a law book in the
temple, it was not Jeremiah who was called into the counsels of the government, but Huldah, a prophetess who
functioned within the dominant system and was a part
of it.[15]

[14] II Kings 9:1 ff.   [15] II Kings 22:14 ff.

In this sense, then, the great prophets seem to be futile men, if one looks only at what they were able to do about influencing contemporary situations. But all that is changed if one considers their relation to progress through the changes that were wrought in the dominant pattern itself as a result of their ministry of criticism. For, through the prophets, the Hebrew people, as a people, developed the faculty of self-criticism which, whether in an individual or in a society, is always a necessary step in cultural progress.

At the outset it was stated that the prophets did not produce single-handed the distinctive religion-culture out of which both Judaism and Christianity later emerged. The system which prevailed in their days, and which had been inherited from hoary antiquity, remained in social control long after the prophetic movement here considered had petered out in frustration. But that system which survived the attack of the prophets became itself their enduring monument. There is no single aspect of it, whether its ideal, or its philosophy, or its institutions, or its literature, which does not testify for the prophetic contribution to progress, for the part they played in making the Hebrew spirit inherently influential and in setting it amarch down the centuries.

Through the impetus they gave, the cultus of the dominant system was gradually purged of sympathetic magic, until the very rituals and myths were made the vehicle of the expression of a higher philosophy, a different way of interpreting the meaning of life. Through the drive of their social ideals the place held by the common man in the brotherhood of Israel was gradually enlarged.

Through the influence of their respect for human intelligence there developed, in the course of centuries, a passion for learning and education, for the part thought and meditation play in culture, which comes to a most noble expression in the first psalm, where "the law of the Lord" is not a mere instrument of social control, but a window that opens on the universe, a door into a larger life.

In much of that which is noble in the Jewish and Christian cultures, as they stand today, the prophetic influence lives. And one may be sure that the nobler cultures which may spring from these in the future will never so far advance as to escape from the aura of the spirit of Israel's prophets. For the prophetic way is a way that is bound up with life. It is of that eternal stuff which does not die.

SELECTED BIBLIOGRAPHY

SELECTED BIBLIOGRAPHY

The list of books and articles presented below hardly merits description as a bibliography. It is included for a twofold purpose: first, to indicate some of the works which the writer has found stimulating and so to compensate for the omission of footnotes; and second, to suggest to the general reader where he may find some materials of which he may make use to enlarge his knowledge of the subject treated. The reader will find a larger and very useful selected bibliography in Chester Charlton McCown, *The Genesis of the Social Gospel*, New York and London: Knopf, 1929, pp. 379 ff., which, in its turn, may be further supplemented from the chapter bibliographies of the *Cambridge Ancient History*, particularly Volumes I–III.

ABBREVIATIONS

AJSL = American Journal of Semitic Languages and Literature. Chicago: University of Chicago Press, 1884—.

AJT = American Journal of Theology. Chicago: University of Chicago Press, 1897–1920.

ERE = Encyclopedia of Religion and Ethics. 13 vols., ed. by James Hastings. New York: Scribner, 1908–27.

JAOS = Journal of the American Oriental Society. New Haven: Yale University Press, 1843—.

JBL = Journal of Biblical Literature. New Haven: Society of Biblical Literature and Exegesis, 1881—.

JEA = Journal of Egyptian Archaeology. London: Egyptian Exploration Fund, 1914—.

JPOS = Journal of the Palestine Oriental Society. Jerusalem: Palestine Oriental Society, 1920—.

JR = Journal of Religion. Chicago: University of Chicago Press, 1921—.

JRAS = Journal of the Royal Asiatic Society of Great Britain and Ireland. London: Royal Asiatic Society, 1834—.

ZAW = Zeitschrift für die alttestamentliche Wissenschaft und die Kunde des nachbiblischen Judentums. Giessen: Töpelmann, 1881—.

THE WORLD

ALBRIGHT, WILLIAM FOXWELL. The Archaeology of Palestine and the Bible. Chicago: Revell, 1932.

———. "The North Canaanite Epic of Al'eyan Baal," JPOS, XII (1932), 185 ff.

ASTING, RAGMAN KRISTIAN. Die Heiligkeit im Urchristentum. Göttingen: Vanderhoeck und Ruprecht, 1930.

BARTON, GEORGE AARON. Sumerian Religious Texts. New Haven: Yale University Press, 1928.

———. "A North Syrian Poem on the Conquest of Death," JAOS, LII (1932), 221 ff.

———. Semitic and Hamitic Origins. Philadelphia: University of Pennsylvania Press, 1934.

———. "A Liturgy for the Spring Festival at Jerusalem in the Age of Abraham and Melchizedek, I" JBL, LIII (1934), 61 ff.

BAUDISSIN, WOLF WILHELM FRIEDRICH, GRAF VON. Adonis und Esmun. Leipzig: Hinrichs, 1911.

BAUER, HANS, "Die Gottheiten von Ras Shamra," ZAW, LI (1933), 81 ff.

BEGRICH, JOACHIM. "Die Paradieserzählung, eine literargeschichtliche Studie," ZAW, L (1932), 81 ff.

BERTHOLET, ALFRED. A History of Hebrew Civilization. Translated by A. K. Dallas. New York: Brentano, 1926.

BEWER, JULIUS AUGUST. "Hellenistic Mystery Religions and the Old Testament," JBL, XLV (1926), 1 ff.

BLACKMAN, AYLWARD MANLEY. "The Rite of Opening the Mouth in Ancient Egypt and Babylonia," JEA, X (1924–25), 47 ff., 249 ff.

————. "Osiris or the Sun God," JEA, XI (1925), 201 ff.

————. Articles "Priest, Priesthood (Egyptian)," and "Worship (Egyptian)," ERE, X, 293 ff., XII, 776 ff.

BREASTED, JAMES HENRY. The Development of Religion and Thought in Ancient Egypt. New York: Scribners, 1912.

————. A History of Egypt. 2d ed. New York: Scribners, 1924.

————. The Dawn of Conscience. New York: Scribners, 1933.

BUDGE, SIR ERNEST ALFRED. Osiris and the Egyptian Resurrection. New York: Putnam, 1911.

————. The Book of the Dead. London: K. Paul, Trench, Trübner. New York: Dutton, 1928.

CADBURY, HENRY JOEL. "Egyptian Influence on the Book of Proverbs," JR, IX (1929), 99 ff.

CASE, SHIRLEY JACKSON. The Evolution of Early Christianity. Chicago: University of Chicago Press, 1914.

CHEYNE, THOMAS KELLY. The Two Religions of Israel. London: A. and C. Black, 1911.

CHILDE, VERE GORDON. The Aryans. New York: Knopf, 1928.

————. New Light on the Most Ancient East. New York: Appleton, 1934.

CONTENAU, GEORGES. La Civilisation Phénicienne. Paris: Payot, 1926.

COOK, STANLEY ARTHUR. The Place of the Old Testament in Modern Research. Cambridge: University Press, 1932.

————. Ethical Monotheism in the Light of Comparative Religion. London: West London Synagogue Association, 1932.

COOKE, GEORGE ALBERT. Text Book of North Semitic Inscriptions. Oxford: Clarendon Press, 1903.

DAWSON, CHRISTOPHER HENRY. The Age of the Gods. Boston: Mifflin. London: J. Murray, 1928.

DHORME, PAUL. "Première des Textes Phéniciens des Ras Shamra." Revue Biblique. Paris: Libr. Victor Lecoffre, XL (1931), 34 ff.

DOUGHTY, CHARLES MONTAGU. Travels in Arabia Deserta. New York: Boni and Liveright, 1926.

DUSSAUD, RENÉ. "La Mythologie Phénicienne d'après des Tablettes de Ras Shamra," Revue de l'histoire des religions. Paris: E. Leroux, CIV (1932), 353 ff.

EISSFELDT, OTTO. "Yahweh as King," ZAW, XLVI (1928), 81 ff.
————. Baal Zaphon. Zeus Kasios, und der Durchgang der Israeliten durchs Meer. Halle: Niemeyer, 1932.
ERMAN, ADOLPH. A Handbook of Egyptian Religion, tr. by A. S. Griffith. London: Constable, 1907.
————. The Literature of the Ancient Egyptians, tr. by Aylward M. Blackman. London: Methuen, 1927.

FARBRIDGE, MAURICE HARRY. Studies in Biblical and Semitic Symbolism. London: K. Paul, Trench, and Trübner. New York: Dutton, 1923.
FRAZER, SIR JAMES GEORGE. Adonis, Attis, Osiris, 2d ed. London: Macmillan, 1907.

GALLING, KURT. Die israelitische Staatsverfassung in ihrer vorderorientalischen Umwelt. Leipzig: Hinrichs, 1929.
GASTER, THEODOR HERZL. "The Combat of Death and the Most High," JRAS, 1932, pp. 857 ff.
————. "The Ritual Pattern of a Ras Shamra Epic," Archiv Orientální, Praha: Orientální ústav, V (1933), 118 ff.
GINSBERG, H. L., and MAISLER, B. "Semitised Ḫurrians in Syria and Palestine," JPOS, XIV (1934), 243 ff.
GODBEY, ALLEN HOWARD. The Lost Tribes, a Myth. Durham, N. C: Duke University Press, 1930.
————. New Light on the Old Testament. Norman, Oklahoma: University Litho., 1934.
GRAHAM, WILLIAM CREIGHTON. "Recent Light on the Cultural Origins of the Hebrews," JR, XIV (1934), 307 ff.
GRAY, GEORGE BUCHANAN. Sacrifice in the Old Testament. Oxford: Clarendon Press, 1925.
GROBEL, WILLIAM KENDRICK. A Preliminary Investigation of the Ancestry of the Irregular Verbs in Hebrew. A.M. dissert., University of Chicago, 1932.

GRUFFYDD, W. J. "Moses in the Light of Comparative Folklore," ZAW, XLVI (1928), 260 ff.

GUNTHER, HANS F. K. Rassenkunde des jüdischen Volkes. München: J. F. Lehmann, 1930.

HEMPEL, JOHANNES. Altes Testament und Geschichte. Gütersloh: C. Bertelsmann, 1930.

HOOKE, SAMUEL HENRY (ed.).[1] Myth and Ritual. London: Oxford University Press, 1933.

JASTROW, MORRIS. Die Religion Babyloniens und Assyriens. Giessen: A. Töpelmann, 1912.

————. "Sumerian Myths of Beginnings," AJSL, XXXIII (1917). 91 ff.

JAYNE, WALTER ADDISON. The Healing Gods of Ancient Civilizations. New Haven: Yale University Press, 1925.

JENSEN, PETER CHRISTIAN ALBRECHT. Gilgamesh-epos, judaische Nationalsagen, Ilias und Odyssee. Leipsig: E. Pfeiffer, 1924.

KRAELING, EMIL GOTTLIEB HEINRICH. "The Real Religion of Ancient Israel," JBL, XLVII (1928), 133 ff.

LANGDON, STEPHEN HERBERT. Semitic Mythology. Boston: Archaelogical Institute of America, Marshall Jones, 1931.

————. The Babylonian Epic of Creation. Oxford: Clarendon Press, 1933.

LODS, ADOLPHE. Israel. Des origines au milieu du VIIIᵉ siècle. Paris: La Renaissance du livre, 1930.

McEWAN, CALVIN WELLS. Oriental Forerunners of Hellenistic Kingship. University of Chicago Ph.D. dissert., 1931.

MATTHEWS, ISAAC GEORGE. "Tammuz Worship in the Book of Malachi," JPOS, XI (1931), 42 ff.

MEEK, THEOPHILE JAMES. "Canticles and the Tammuz Cult," AJSL, XXXIX (1922), 1 ff.

[1] The author has been informed by Professor Hooke that a volume entitled *The Labyrinth* will shortly be published. This work will also be an important contribution to the subject.

MEEK, THEOPHILE JAMES. "Babylonian Parallels to the Song of Songs," JBL, XLIII (1924), 245 ff.

———. "Light from the Old Testament on Primitive Religion," Canadian Journal of Religious Thought, Toronto, Canada, II (1925), 32–36.

———. "The Interpenetration of Cultures as Illustrated by the Character of the Old Testament Literature," JR, VII (1927), 244 ff.

MENES, ABRAM. Die vorexilischen Gesetze Israels im Zusammenhang seiner kulturgeschichtlichen Entwicklung. Giessen: A. Töpelmann, 1928.

MONTGOMERY, JAMES ALLEN. "The Wailing of Hadad-Rimmon (Zech. 12:11)," JBL, XXXIII (1914), 78 ff.

MORGENSTERN, JULIAN. "Two Ancient Israelite Agricultural Festivals," Jewish Quarterly Review, Philadelphia: Dropsie College, VIII (1917), 31 ff.

———. "Origin of the Massoth," AJT, XXII (1917), 27 ff.

MOWINCKEL, SIGMUND. Die Psalmenstudien. Kristiania: J. Dybwad, 1921.

———. "Der Ursprung der Bilaamsage," ZAW, LXVIII (1930), 233 ff.

MURRAY, MARGARET ALICE. "The Dying God," in Ancient Egypt, XIII, London–New York: Macmillan, 1928, pp. 8 ff.

NORTH, C. R. "The Religious Aspects of Hebrew Kingship," ZAW, L (1932), 8 ff.

OLMSTEAD, ALBERT TEN EYCK. History of Assyria. New York: Scribners, 1923.

———. History of Palestine and Syria. New York: Scribners, 1931.

PATON, LEWIS BAYLES. "The Cult of the Mother Goddess in Ancient Palestine," Biblical World, Chicago: Hebrew Book Exchange, XXXVI (1910), 26 ff.

PEAKE, ARTHUR SAMUEL. The People and the Book. Oxford: Clarendon Press, 1925.

PEDERSEN, JOHANNES. Israel: Its Life and Culture. London: Oxford University Press, 1926.

———. "Die Auffassung vom Alten Testament," ZAW, XLIX (1931), 161 ff.

PETERS, JOHN P. "The Worship of Tammuz," JBL, XXVI (1917), 100 ff.

———. "Notes and Suggestions on the Early Sumerian Religion and Its Expression," JAOS, XLI (1921), 131 ff.

PETRIE, WILLIAM MATTHEW FLINDERS. "Osiris in the Tree and Pillar," Ancient Egypt, Vol. XII. London–New York: Macmillan, 1928.

PFISTER, FRIEDRICH. Art. "Kultus" in Pauly-Wissowa, Realencyclopädie der classischen Altertumwissenschaft, Vol. 22. Stuttgart: J. B. Metzlersche, 1922.

PHILBY, HARRY ST. JOHN BRIDGER. The Heart of Arabia. New York: Putnam, 1923.

ROGERS, ROBERT WILLIAMS. Cuneiform Parallels to the Old Testament. 2d ed. Cincinnati: Abingdon, 1926.

SCHOFF, WILFRED HARVEY (ed.). The Song of Songs, a Symposium. Philadelphia: Commercial Museum, 1924.

SHARPE, JOHN. The Tree of Life. Cambridge: Deighton Bell, 1889.

SMITH, JOHN MERLIN POWIS. "Traces of Emperor Worship in the Old Testament," AJSL, XXXIX (1922), 32 ff.

———. "The Indebtedness of Israel to Its Neighbors," AJSL, XLIX (1933), 172 ff.

SMITH, SIDNEY. Early History of Assyria. London: Chatto and Windus, 1928.

SMITH, WILLIAM ROBERTSON. Lectures on the Religion of the Semites, the Fundamental Institutions, edited by Stanley Arthur Cook. London: A. and C. Black, 1927.

SPEISER, EPHRAIM AVIGDOR. Mesopotamian Origins. Philadelphia: University of Pennsylvania Press, 1930.

STRONG, HERBERT AUGUSTUS. The Syrian Goddess, a Translation of Lucian's De dea Syria. London: Constable, 1913.

TAYLOR, THOMAS GRIFFITH. Environment and Race. London: Oxford University Press, 1927.

THUREAU-DANGIN, FRANÇOIS. Rituels Accadienne. Paris: E. Leroux, 1921.

VELLAY, CHARLES. Le Culte et les Fêtes d'Adonis-Thammouz. Paris: E. Leroux, 1904.

VIROLLEAUD, CHARLES. "The Gods of Phoenicia as Revealed by the Poem of Ras Shamra," Antiquity, Gloucester, England, V (1931), 405.

——. "Les Cultes Phéniciens et Syriens au IIe Millénaire avant l'Ere Chrétienne," Journal des Savants, XXIX (1931), 164 ff.

WILLIAMS, WALTER GEORGE. The Ras Shamra Inscriptions and Israel's Cultural Heritage. University of Chicago Ph.D. dissert., 1934.

WOOD, WILLIAM CARLETON. "The Religion of Canaan," JBL, XXXV (1916), 1 ff., 163 ff.

WOOLEY, CHARLES LEONARD. The Sumerians. Oxford: Clarendon Press, 1928.

THE PROPHETS

BADÈ, WILLIAM FREDERIC. The Old Testament in the Light of To-day. Boston–New York: Mifflin, 1915.

BERTHOLET, ALFRED. Die Religion des Alten Testaments. Tübingen: J. C. B. Mohr, 1932.

——. Das Dynamistische im Alten Testament. Tübingen: J. C. B. Mohr, 1926.

BLUNT, ALFRED WALTER FRANK. The Prophets of Israel. Oxford: Clarendon Press, 1929.

BUTTENWIESER, MOSES. The Prophets of Israel. New York: Macmillan, 1914.

CADBURY, HENRY JOEL. National Ideals in the Old Testament. New York: Scribners, 1920.

CASE, SHIRLEY JACKSON. The Millenial Hope. Chicago: University of Chicago Press, 1918.

COOK, STANLEY ARTHUR. The Religion of Ancient Palestine in the Light of Archaeology. London: Oxford University Press (published for the British Academy by H. Milford), 1930.

COSSMAN, WILLY. Die Entwicklung des Gerichts-gedankens bei Alten-testamentlichen Propheten. Giessen: A. Töpelmann, 1915.

DRIVER, SAMUEL ROLLES. The Ideals of the Prophets. Edinburgh: T. and T. Clark, 1915.

FULLERTON, KEMPER. Prophecy and Authority. New York: Macmillan, 1919.

GRAHAM, WILLIAM CREIGHTON. "Notes on the Interpretation of Isaiah 5:1 ff.," AJSL, XLV (1929), 167 ff.
———. "The Religion of the Hebrews," JR, XI (1931), 242 ff.
———. "Some Suggestions toward the Interpretation of Micah 1:10–16," AJSL, XLVII (1931), 237 ff.
———. "Isaiah's Part in the Syro-Ephraimitic Crisis," AJSL, L (1934), 201 ff.

GRESSMANN, HUGO. Der Ursprung der Israelitisch-jüdischen Eschatologie. Göttingen: Vanderhoeck und Ruprecht, 1905.
———. Der Messias. Göttingen: Vanderhoeck und Ruprecht, 1905.

GUNKEL, HERMANN. Die Propheten. Göttingen: Vanderhoeck und Ruprecht, 1917.

HERTZBERG, HANS WILHELM. Prophet und Gott, eine Studie zur Religiosität des Vor-exilischen Prophetums. Gütersloh: C. Bertelsmann, 1923.

IRWIN, WILLIAM ANDREW. "The Thinking of Amos," AJSL, XLIX (1933), 102 ff.

JEPSEN, ALFRED. Nabi. Soziologische Studien zur alttestamentlichen Literatur und Religionsgeschichte. München: C. H. Beck'sche, 1924.

KELLERMANN, BENZION. Der Ethische Monotheismus der Propheten und seine Soziologische Würdigung. Berlin: C. A. Schwetschke, 1917.

KENT, CHARLES FOSTER. Makers and Teachers of Judaism. New York: Scribners, 1911.

KINCHELOE, SAMUEL CLARENCE. The Prophet, a Study in the Sociology of Leadership. University of Chicago Ph.D. dissert., 1929.

KITTEL, RUDOLPH. The Religion of the People of Israel. New York: Macmillan, 1925.

———. Great Men and Movements in Israel, tr. by Charlotte A. Knoch and C. D. Wright. New York: Macmillan, 1929.

McCONNELL, FRANCIS JOHN. The Prophetic Ministry. Abingdon Press, 1930.

McCOWN, CHESTER CHARLTON. The Genesis of the Social Gospel. New York: Knopf, 1929.

McFADYEN, JOHN EDGAR. Introduction to the Old Testament. New York: Armstrong. London: Hodder and Stoughton, 1906.

———. The Message of Israel. London: J. Clarke, 1932.

MAY, HERBERT GORDON. "The Evolution of the Joseph Story," AJSL, XLVII (1931), 83 ff.

———. Hosea and Israel's Cult. University of Chicago Ph.D. dissert., 1932.

———. "The Fertility Cult in Hosea," AJSL, XVIII (1932), 73 ff.

———. The Material Remains of the Megiddo Cult. Oriental Institute Publications, XXVI (in press), Chicago.

MEEK, THEOPHILE JAMES. "A Proposed Reconstruction of Early Hebrew History," AJT, XXIV (1920), 209 ff.

———. "Some Religious Origins of the Hebrews," AJSL, XXXVII (1921), 101 ff.

———. "Aaronites and Zadokites," AJSL, XLV (1929), 149 ff.

———. "Some Old Testament Problems in the Light of Recent Archaeological Discoveries," Canadian Journal of Religious Thought, Toronto, Canada, VI (1929), 374 ff.

NORTH, C. R. "The Old Testament Estimate of the Monarchy," AJSL, XLVIII (1931), 1 ff.

NOYES, CARLETON ELDREDGE. The Genius of Israel. Boston–New York: Mifflin, 1924.

OESTERLEY, WILLIAM OSCAR EMIL, and THEODORE HENRY ROBINSON. Hebrew Religion. London: Society for Promoting Christian Knowledge. New York–Toronto: Macmillan, 1930.

PFEIFFER, ROBERT HENRY. "The Polemic against Idolatry in the Old Testament," JBL, XLIII (1924), 229 ff.

POVAH, JOHN WALTER. The New Psychology and the Hebrew Prophets. London, New York, etc.: Longmans, Green, 1925.

RAD, GERHARD VON. "Die Falschen Propheten," ZAW, LI (1933), 109 ff.

ROBINSON, THEODORE HENRY. Prophecy and the Prophets in Ancient Israel. London: Duckworth. New York: Scribners, 1923.

SELLIN, ERNST. Das Zwölfprophetenbuch, in Kommentar zum Alten Testament. Leipzig: Deichertsche, 1929.

SKINNER, JOHN. Prophecy and Religion. Cambridge: University Press, 1932.

SMITH, SIR GEORGE ADAM. The Book of the Twelve Prophets. New York: Armstrong, 1898.

SMITH, HENRY PRESERVED. The Religion of Israel. New York: Scribners, 1914.

SMITH, JOHN MERLIN POWIS. The Prophet and His Problems. New York: Scribners, 1914.

——. The Moral Life of the Hebrews. Chicago: University of Chicago Press, 1923.

——. The Prophets and Their Times. Chicago: University of Chicago Press, 1925.

——. "The Growth of the Hebrew Idea of God," JR, XII (1932), 24 ff.

TORREY, CHARLES CUTLER. "The Prophecy of Malachi," JBL, XVII (1898), 1 ff.

WALLIS, LOUIS. Sociological Study of the Bible. Chicago: University of Chicago Press, 1912.

———. God and the Social Process. Chicago: University of Chicago Press, 1934.

WELCH, ADAM CLEGHORN. The Religion of Israel under the Kingdom. Edinburgh: T. and T. Clark, 1912.

WOLVERTON, WALLACE IRVING. Amos as a Thinker. University of Chicago A.M. dissert., 1932.

CONCLUSION

BARNES, HENRY ELMER. The New History and the Social Studies. New York: Century, 1925.

BOWER, WILLIAM CLAYTON. Religion and the Good Life. New York, Cincinnati, etc.: Abingdon Press, 1933.

CASE, SHIRLEY JACKSON. Social Origins of Christianity. Chicago: University of Chicago Press, 1923.

DAWSON, CHRISTOPHER HENRY. Progress and Religion. London: Sheed and Ward, 1931.

ELLWOOD, CHARLES ABRAM. Cultural Evolution. New York–London: Century, 1927.

EMERSON, RALPH WALDO. An Address to the Senior Class in Divinity College, Cambridge, July 11, 1838, in Nature Addresses and Lectures. Boston–Cambridge: J. Munroe, 1849.

FAIRCHILD, HENRY PRATT. The Foundations of Social Life. New York: J. Wiley. London: Chapman and Hall, 1927.

GRAHAM, WILLIAM CREIGHTON. "Religion and Human Worth," JR (1930), 495 ff.

HOCKING, WILLIAM ERNEST. "What Is a Lost Soul?" Chicago Theological Seminary Register, XXIII (1933), 9 f.

MATHEWS, SHAILER. The Church and the Changing Order. New York: Macmillan, 1907.

———. The Social Gospel. Philadelphia, Boston, etc.: The Griffith and Rowland Press, 1910.

————. The Spiritual Interpretation of History. Cambridge: Harvard University Press, 1916.

————. The Faith of Modernism. New York: Macmillan, 1924.

————. Jesus on Social Institutions. New York: Macmillan, 1928.

————. Growth of the Idea of God. New York: Macmillan, 1932.

————. Christianity and Social Process. New York: Harper, 1934.

MURRAY, GILBERT. Tradition and Progress. Boston–New York: Mifflin, 1922.

WIEMAN, HENRY NELSON. The Wrestle of Religion with Truth. New York: Macmillan, 1927.

INDEX

INDEX